TRAVIS WAUGH

FULLY COMPLIAN

COMPLIANCE
TRAINING
TO CHANGE
BEHAVIOR

ATD Press is an internationally renowned source of insightful and practical information on talent development, training, and professional development.

ATD Press
1640 King Street
Alexandria, VA 22314 USA

Ordering information: Books published by ATD Press can be purchased by visiting ATD's website at www.td.org/books or by calling 800.628.2783 or 703.683.8100.

Library of Congress Control Number: 2019941225

ISBN-10: 1-947308-35-1
ISBN-13: 978-1-947308-35-0
e-ISBN: 978-1-947308-36-7

ATD Press Editorial Staff
Director: Sarah Halgas
Manager: Melissa Jones
Community of Practice Manager, Learning & Development: Eliza Blanchard
Developmental Editor: Jack Harlow
Text Design: Shirley E.M. Raybuck
Cover Design: Lindy Martin, Faceout Studio
Printed by Versa Press, East Peoria, IL

Contents

Acknowledgments

This book can only begin with a sincere thank you to the many individuals whose perspective made it possible. I've been creating compliance training courses and tutorials for more than a decade, but without the other voices found in this book, I would have little worth writing on the subject, and even less worth reading.

In addition to the venerable experts who graciously agreed to be interviewed for this book, and the researchers whose work offered evidence-based suggestions for influencing employee behavior and measurably reducing misconduct, the pages to come are influenced heavily by the individual learning and compliance practitioners that I've had the opportunity to commiserate with in recent years.

The best part of speaking, writing, and facilitating courses on compliance has been the chance to meet these thoughtful people and see that we are all struggling with the exact same issues. All of us have experienced a stubborn SME who insists on adding more and more legal content to an already bloated tutorial, instead of boiling the message down to its most relevant components. We all know the feeling of reading a dry policy or law and struggling to imagine how it will ever become an engaging or useful course. We've all sat through a tutorial that we know is doing nothing more than checking a box, and we know how frustrating that can be.

These shared conversations provide much-needed emotional support and encouragement, allowing us all to return to the office rejuvenated, reminded that we are not alone, and ready to keep fighting for the worthy cause of better, more relevant compliance. I could not have written this book confidently unless I knew that I wasn't speaking only for myself. I believe that the opinions found on the following pages are the opinions of every well-intentioned learning and development professional who has found themselves forced to compromise on what they know is best for their learners, in the name of some abstract sense of required compliance. Hopefully, this book will offer tangible techniques that can help shift that compromise in the future, allowing us to continue meeting the letter of the law, but only in a way that course developers can feel proud of and participants can genuinely learn from. With a strategic approach and a dogged commitment, we can help our organizations quit using compliance training only to comply, and start using it to make a real difference.

To all these noble practitioners, I say thank you for your continued efforts to make compliance training the best that it can be. Hopefully this book will help.

Finally, I'd like to thank my wife, who gave me the time and space to write this book during the same year we prepared for and welcomed our first child. I dedicate this book to him, in hopes that his generation will never know what it feels like to suffer through a boring, irrelevant compliance tutorial.

Introduction

The Call for a Better Kind of Compliance

In a Dallas conference room in 2017, a large group of likeminded professionals gathered to discuss learning and development at their organizations. The event was dubbed a "learning best practices forum," and there was no shortage of best practices on display. Proud teams shared snippets from their latest online tutorials—including branching ethical scenarios, game show parodies, and evocative true stories—all featuring professional actors, tight scripts, and polished production value. Other groups shared how they had weaved their employees' learning needs seamlessly into their internal systems and onboarding processes, or branched their learning paths to focus each learner on relevant, timely content that maximized their limited attention. A team from a large computer manufacturer revealed a custom-built video game that combined the priorities of a new company-wide initiative with material on core sales and management skills and a slew of required compliance subjects. The game provided a challenging, highly interactive experience in which the learners encountered everything they were required to learn in a context that felt realistic, useful, and fun.

At the end of each presentation, the audience cheered and congratulated their peers. The participant questions were knowledgeable and engaged, showing the audience's eagerness to absorb the lessons on display and apply them back in the workplace. It was the kind of gratifying, reaffirming focus on learners and learning that one might expect from an Association for Talent Development conference filled with instructional designers and learning professionals. Only these attendees weren't learning professionals. They were lawyers.

Welcome to the Ethics and Compliance Initiative's two-day Training Best Practices Forum for head legal counsels, compliance officers, risk management directors, and auditors. These attendees are the subject matter experts charged with ensuring organizational compliance, and for whom completion percentages and participation hours were once the only learning metric for which they would be judged. And yet, they readily applauded the learner-centered approach on display over those two days in Dallas, and they left demanding more.

Understanding who these people are, and why they'd chosen to spend those two days together in Dallas, can tell us a lot about the state of compliance training today, and provide a telling glimpse of where it's headed. But before we peek too far ahead, let's clarify exactly what compliance training is.

A Working Definition

In many organizations, compliance training has become an umbrella term for everything we feel compelled by some external entity to teach our employees. This single word, *compelled*, may best capture the essence of how we and our learners intuitively experience compliance training courses and tutorials: These are the subjects we have been *compelled* to teach and learn, whether we want to or not.

Unfortunately, this sense of obligation has pervaded the tone and quality of most compliance training content developed over the last several decades, especially as the coinciding boom of e-learning technologies has allowed the learning profession to soak audiences with irrelevant content more efficiently than ever before. However, reducing the definition of compliance training to merely *required training* does not capture the intention at the heart of most compliance mandates, nor does it capture the real value that compliance training could and should deliver to organizations.

In practice, organizations create many compliance training courses to avoid the legal risk of failing to comply with a specific legal mandate. However, that's just one of the risks that good compliance training should strive to address, and it's not true that everything currently called "compliance training" has been specifically mandated by some regulatory agency or law. To account for the full scope of modern compliance, we need a broader definition.

Instead, the following definition can explain the phrase *compliance training* as it will be used as shorthand throughout this book: Compliance training is any learning course or program designed to manage a specific legal risk *and* cultivate an ethical and accountable culture.

Whether required by law or not, any training course or tutorial may be considered compliance if it has been implemented primarily to manage the risk of unsafe, unethical, or unjust behavior in the workplace, and the dramatic costs such behaviors can generate. This risk is managed through specific training—a course on how to responsibly make a purchase or trade stocks or protect customers' private data, for example. It is also managed more broadly, by building a culture in which all employees are accountable and empowered to make sound ethical decisions.

Any training program designed primarily to manage risk, whether legal or ethical, will lend itself to the same predictable challenges and opportunities, which we will explore throughout this book.

Beyond One Form of Training

While this working definition offers sufficient focus for our conversation, it also provides flexibility by not restraining our discussion to a particular form of training. Tutorials and other online training formats will be a frequent topic of discussion due to their prevalent use in addressing large-scale compliance training needs, but the core tips we will explore should be equally relevant to in-person classes, webinars, informal training, microlearning, or any other form of learning and development best suited to your audience and organization.

Competing Terms

It's worth noting, from the breadth of our working definition, that not all compliance training is actually about compliance, at least not in the sense of complying with a specific policy or law. Code of conduct or ethical behavior training is often lumped in with compliance, even though they're seldom mandated by an external agency or a specific law. In certain cases, it can be difficult to see what a good compliance course was created to comply with.

Good compliance officers are building learning and compliance programs that serve a higher, broader purpose than merely ensuring organizational adherence to predetermined and mandated requirements. Instead, they are trying to build robust, resilient cultures that are capable of regulating themselves.

Indeed, many compliance professionals now hasten to brand their industry as Ethics and Compliance or Ethics and Governance or simply Risk Management, and opt for titles like chief integrity officer or senior ethics champion, which focus more on the culture and behaviors they are trying to cultivate and less on the mandates with which they are trying to comply. However, while integrity learning or ethics learning may be a more fitting title for our ultimate aspirations, the phrase *compliance training* is still ubiquitous in the learning industry for describing all manner of required tutorials and courses. To capitalize on this familiarity, we will use this term throughout this book.

The Problem With Traditional Compliance Training

The compliance experts who gathered that week in Dallas had all cleared their busy calendars and flown to Texas to solve a problem—one that threatened to alienate them from their organizations, marginalize their best laid plans, and render their traditional programs ineffective. That problem was training.

Compliance training, as traditionally implemented in many organizations, contains three existential flaws that will require a dramatic change of approach in the years ahead: It's unsustainable, it's detrimental to behavior, and it's failing to effectively manage risk.

Unsustainable

Adding a new course or new tutorial to address every new policy, risk, or legislative action may have once felt like a responsible risk management strategy. After all, you wouldn't want your employees to make a costly mistake, only to discover that your company's training programs had never addressed the subject. Without an applicable course in place, your company's legal defense may crumble as you're unable to claim in court that the bad actor should have known better. The corporation ignored the risk, a lawyer or judge might argue, and that negligence could make you collectively responsible for what comes next.

As we'll explore in part 1, these legal pressures create a strong incentive to include more courses in our catalogs and more details in each course. But even if the exhaustive approach makes sense from a lawyer's risk management point of view—which we'll soon see it might not—it's no longer tenable as a realistic option. There are simply too many compliance subjects in our complex, global economy than we could ever address for every member of our audience. The idea of "hitting everything" is simply impossible, unless we want to dedicate our full business strategy to compliance, leaving no time for selling, or manufacturing, or whatever else it is you've actually hired your employees to do.

To thrive in this rapidly evolving compliance landscape, we're going to have to make more strategic decisions about what to train, when, and who needs training, even when that training is mandatory. One-size-fits-all learning was never really possible in the first place, but the growing scope of compliance is making that more obvious at every level of our organizations.

Detrimental to Behavior

The huge scope of corporate compliance subjects, and the pressure to create exhaustive training as a means of preparing a potential legal defense, has necessitated some less-than-ideal courses. And those compromises have taken a toll on our learners.

We all know how time consuming and potentially costly proper user analysis can be. It takes time to get out and work with users to determine what they really need. Unfortunately, the constant flood of new compliance subjects has left little time for any meaningful dialogue with the people who will ultimately be subjected to our training. Instead, we take the slides and notes from a subject matter expert, pretty them up the best we can, implement the course and enroll as many users as possible, and move on as quickly as we can to the next course in the long list of compliance subjects that demand our learning and development attention.

If that sounds familiar, you're likely not surprised to hear that not all these courses are hitting the mark. Instead, learners see compliance as little more than a calculated exercise to protect their company's leadership from future blame. They believe that they are only an afterthought in the compliance endeavor, and far too often, they are right.

Unsurprisingly, this old brand of compliance is terrible for morale, and counter-productive at decreasing the behaviors it's ostensibly designed to address. As *Slate* magazine summarized from a 1999 study of 10,000 employees across six organizations, ethics and compliance programs that employees believe are intended "only to protect top management from blame" are the least effective in achieving their stated goals. Employees can easily surmise their executives' motivation for the training from the program's tone and structure, and if that motivation appears to be only self-preservation, those employees will "ignore, or even rebel against, the lessons of the training" (Anderson 2016).

Failing to Effectively Manage Risk

A legal defense is only as strong as its weakest link. Unfortunately, for many compliance-based risk management programs the weakest link is often training.

Even if your organization has great policies and enforcement mechanisms, a training course or tutorial that shows a lack of investment, regard for the learner, or behavioral purpose could undermine the credibility of everything else your compliance team has put in place. This company was clearly only checking a box for the sake of checking a box, a savvy judge may deduce, and that doubt may prompt dangerous cynicism toward your entire program.

Indeed, the most intelligent policies, laws, and official guidance are already asking for more than mere training, as we will explore in the following chapters. Laws that truly hope to change behavior are asking for "rigorous" and "effective" training in an effort to prevent the lip-service tutorials of the past. These progressive laws state that training can't just exist, but that it must be proven effective through measurement or an appeal to established pedagogical best practices. Think of all the compliance tutorials you've sat through as a participant in your career. How many would meet either of those measures?

Through the years, the compliance training programs that many organizations have employed have become too much about compliance, and not nearly enough about learning. While preparing your company to win a legal defense or mitigate the cost of a settlement is nice, wouldn't it be better to stay out of court in the first place? Instead of training that allows us to say "See, we told them not to," what if we could tell them not to in a way they could hear and apply? Wouldn't it be nice to actually change behavior?

How This Book Will Help

Learning professionals have been boasting for years that we hold the keys to real behavior change, and at least some compliance officers are starting to take note.

By skipping out on analysis, design, and evaluation, quick and cheap compliance courses have been successful only at mitigating risk after misconduct occurs. If we want to deliver the kind of value that justifies the continued existence of learning and development, we have to build learning experiences that change real behavior, helping our compliance officers avoid risk by diminishing the chance of misconduct in the first place.

Luckily, as learning and development professionals, we already have all the tools we need to succeed. By putting the learner first, and focusing on proven pedagogical principles, we can prepare our organizations to proactively reduce risk by changing behavior. Instead of treating misconduct as inevitable and seeing training only as a tool to mitigate its costs, we can view misconduct as a problem that can be solved, and turn training into a real solution.

But we can't forget our lawyers, compliance officers, and subject matter experts in the process. Their needs are still valid, their budgets still foot the bill for much of our compliance work, and they still need our help to remain compliant with current policies and laws.

Before we can build something better, we'll need the trust of these key compliance partners, which means we must understand the underlying fears and motivations that drive the design of traditional compliance programs. Part 1 of this book provides that legal foundation, starting with a more thorough look at our unique moment in the history of compliance. By understanding the role that compliance training has traditionally played in responsible risk management, learning professionals can build great new solutions that give our learners what they want, without sacrificing what our compliance subject matter experts need.

With the legal constraints established, part 2 focuses on how we can design learner-centered solutions within those constraints that achieve far more than checking boxes and meeting the letter of the law. By unearthing relevant needs and building behavioral solutions that alter our learners' context, habit, and motivation, we can measurably reduce misconduct and generate far greater return on our compliance investment.

Finally, in part 3, we consider the future of compliance training, and how you can position your organization to continue building on the strong behavioral foundation you will establish in the years ahead. Compliance programs may look very different a decade from now, and learning professionals must help shape that future if we hope to serve the best interests of our learners.

Ultimately, the aim of this book is to achieve a balance between the letter of the law and its spirit, between the sensible protections of good regulations and the free agency of our employees, between our commitment to ethical conduct and our drive to succeed in our core business, whatever it may be. Great compliance training can serve all these needs at once, and it must. When we learn to strike the perfect balance between the law and our learners—as outlined in the following chapters—we can start to make a real difference.

Part 1
THE LAW

Chapter 1

The Relatively Recent History of Compliance

There was a time, not very long ago, when companies were encouraged to do basically whatever they wanted to turn a profit. The barons of the Industrial Revolution were not known for their sense of fairness, safety, or social justice. Buyer beware was the order of the day, and both employees and consumers were expected to navigate the jungle the best they could, on their own.

At the turn of the 20th century, working conditions were atrocious, consumer protections were nonexistent, and the backroom deals of crony capitalism were what it meant to do business. In a global culture absent of any meaningful regulation, prices were fixed or gouged at will, food and drugs were often contaminated, and a simple day's work was a perilous fight for survival. It was, by modern standards, an unjust and irresponsible society. And from that rampant injustice sprung an appetite for change.

The 20th century saw industrial economies in Europe, Asia, and America begin a slew of reforms designed to improve public welfare and working conditions and, more cynically, to placate growing civil unrest among their populations. The resulting century-long rise in regulatory oversight has had a direct impact on nearly every modern industry. Even behaviors that are not directly regulated by specific laws or policies have been affected by this shifting perspective on corporate accountability, as the success of earlier laws have engendered a sense in the general populace that society can and should be fair, and that organizations and individuals that act negligently or unfairly can and should face consequences.

Broadly speaking, today's approach to ethics and compliance can be seen as a gradual trajectory from lower order needs to higher order needs, as our society gradually solved or mitigated old problems and shifted its collective attention to new challenges. For example, our current struggles to achieve equal pay for women and reduce sexual harassment would not be up for discussion if we had not already succeeded in securing the right to vote for women and begun to integrate the workplace. Similarly, if gender disparities and harassment ever become less vexing problems, we will likely uncover previously unnoticed injustices for our society to debate and eventually resolve. The arc of history is long, as Martin Luther King Jr. famously said, but it bends toward justice.

This collective progress wasn't quick or easy, and it isn't always uniform. Governments and organizations may roll out well-intentioned policies and laws to address the most pressing misconduct of their day, only to see their successors roll back those regulations in the name of corporate freedom or individual accountability. In any given moment, the culture around us may appear to be rising to unprecedented heights, or backsliding to new lows. But when seen in the long view, this much is clear: Our collective expectations of corporate conduct have ascended dramatically over the last century, and the cost of misconduct has risen with it.

That progress hasn't come without a price. Compliance laws and regulations over the last several decades have proven largely effective in reducing the most egregious cases of corporate corruption and fraud. But in the process, they have inadvertently created a set of rules that don't always prompt the desired results. Instead, they have created a risk management game that too many organizations can choose to play the wrong way and still win.

Nowhere is this twin balance of real progress and counter-productive incentives more apparent than in the seminal piece of legislation that still serves as a boogieman for today's compliance officers: The Federal Sentencing Guidelines of 1991.

The Organization on Trial

How severely should a person be punished for shoplifting? What about speeding? What about murder? And how standardized should those sentences be?

On one hand, an ethical arbitrator may suggest that all sentences should be completely standardized. Shoplifting is shoplifting, after all. Shouldn't all shoplifters receive the same, fair punishment?

Not so fast, another well-intentioned judge may counter. Fairness and consistency are important legal considerations, but not all crimes are created equal. The fairest sentence for one shoplifting offense may not be the fairest sentence for another. To be truly fair, a sentence should take a range of considerations into account, including what was stolen, why it was stolen, how often the individual has stolen in the past, and how likely they are to steal again in the future.

If you live in a modern democracy, you may find this flexibility more comforting than a draconian system where absolute, irrefutable punishments are set in stone for every crime. Context obviously matters in everything we do, and there is some intuitive appeal to a sentencing structure that allows for the full complexity of life. Unfortunately, complexity brings subjectivity, which brings the potential for bias. An example of this potential bias is the well-documented disparity in U.S. court sentences for similar drug violations between different races.

In addition to bias and racism, subjectivity presents other issues for our legal system. Even well-intentioned, unbiased judges could interpret the same facts of the same case in two very different ways, prompting two dramatically different sentences. Because judicial opinion holds such great weight in our legal system, the sentence you receive could be based less on what you did than on which judge happens to be presiding on the bench. Such randomness and luck can feel anything but fair.

It would be wrong to suggest that America has solved its sentencing problem, but it took a major step toward consistency with the passage of the Federal Sentencing Guidelines in 1984. Along with an acceptable range of punishments for specific crimes, the standards included a rubric of mitigating and aggravating factors that judges could use to adjust their sentences. Now, at the end of each trial, judges would be left to tally points on a standardized scorecard to determine how severely or leniently their punishment should fall within the defined range. Some of the points on that scorecard could still allow for subjectivity, which is a problem that several subsequent amendments have tried to address, but at least there was a standardized blueprint for sentencing that lawyers and judges could debate and that defendants across the country could trust.

After a string of high-profile corruption cases in the 1980s, lawmakers saw an opportunity to expand the guidelines as a tool to address corporate behavior. The Guidelines for Organizational Sentencing, passed in 1991, served two primary purposes:

- They gave the organization more skin in the game. With clear-cut penalties and fines for each type of infraction, organizations could see the real dollar value of the behaviors they'd been allowing to occur.
- They established acceptable standards for an effective corporate compliance culture, by including mitigating and aggravating factors that incentivized response and prevention practices. Penalties were adjusted up or down depending on how much, or how little, the organization had done to manage the risk.

After defining a clear carrot and stick, the sentencing guidelines gave organizations the freedom and power to self-regulate and manage their risk as they would any other aspect of their bottom line. This reform was impressively effective, largely eliminating the egregious types of fraud, waste, and abuse that were ubiquitous in the 1980s. But by clearly outlining the rules for which organizations would be judged, it also offered a blueprint for how organizations could mitigate the costs of misconduct, whether or not they actually tried that hard to prevent the misconduct in the first place. These rules gave rise to the traditional compliance program, which has yielded great benefits to many organizations, but also produced some unintended consequences.

By defining the mitigating and aggravating factors so plainly, the guidelines created a scorecard for a game that any organization could play and win relatively easily. In the process, they sketched an outline for the modern corporate compliance program, which is still in place at most organizations today.

The Seven Pillars of the Traditional Compliance Program

The seven pillars of the traditional compliance program, lifted directly from the wording of the sentencing guidelines, are often interpreted literally and implemented directly as an organization's primary risk management strategy. They are:

- clear policies and standards
- executive leadership
- reporting channels for misconduct
- regular monitoring and audits
- incentives and performance management
- proactive training and communication
- appropriate response and prevention.

There is nothing wrong with the pillars themselves, or with the results they have achieved. However, they are also responsible for most of compliance training's worst problems. In their clarity and absoluteness, they make it too easy for executives and compliance officers to confuse the means with the ends, focusing all their efforts on managing legal risk by complying with these seven pieces of guidance, instead of trying to influence behavior and meet the spirit that gave rise to the guidance.

Worse still, by dialing up the costs of ignoring risk, the guidelines created a sort of risk management arms race, where every risk is identified and addressed with the same comprehensive set of tools, prompting more policies, more executive committees, more reports, and more required training. As a direct result, we are now drowning our learners in a sea of compliance training.

And the compliance training boom shows no sign of abating.

The Scope of Modern Compliance Training

The modern organization must manage many risks. Each new mistake that captures the wrong kind of headline seems to demand a new training course, while responses to old mistakes remain entrenched forever in legacy tutorials. The result? An ever-expanding genre of compliance training that fills corporate learning catalogs beyond their effective capacity.

In their 2015 Cost of Compliance Survey, Thomson Reuters warned of regulatory fatigue in the face of increasing, sometimes overlapping domestic and international rules. The survey revealed concern from compliance officers over their ability to meet increasing compliance demands and their anxiety over the personal liability they could face by failing to fully comply.

At the Georgia Institute of Technology alone, where I work as an instructional technologist, a recent campus survey revealed 71 separate compliance training subjects. This is a nearly impossible target to meet effectively, especially given the constraints of the average training and development budget and the available time for employees to step away from work for training. And that's not even to mention the burden that 71 compliance courses would place on our learners' finite and overtaxed attention spans.

If we have any hope of success in crafting compliance training programs that better meet the real needs of our learners and our organizations, we need to find opportunities to consolidate subjects and reduce redundancies between courses. To begin making the right connections, we must understand the scope of compliance training in its broadest sense.

While specific laws and policies may be countless and continuously shifting, especially across countries and industries, the same seven themes emerge again and again—consumer protections, employee protections, civility and diversity, responsible stewardship, fraud and corruption, data privacy and cyber security, and ethics and integrity. When we talk about using compliance training as a tool to reduce misconduct, we're talking about making a measurable difference in one or more of these seven areas. If we get all seven right, we have little to fear as an organization. But a single poor decision, habit, or mistake in any one of these categories can be devastating to an organization's mission.

The Seven Central Themes of Modern Compliance

In the modern organization, compliance training is typically implemented to manage risk in these seven core areas of organizational accountability.

Consumer Protections

Modern compliance subjects include courses on food handling and sanitation, truth in advertising, required financial disclosures for loans and investments, requirements for safe materials in manufacturing, and patient safety regulations for pharmaceutical companies and health care providers.

Employee Protections

Modern compliance subjects include the broad range of employee safety courses mandated by groups like the Occupational Safety and Health Administration (OSHA). They also include Fair Labor Standard Act (FLSA) courses regarding overtime regulation and hour reporting, child labor laws, the right to take job-protected leaves for qualified reasons as established by the Family Medical Leave Act (FMLA), and due-cause protections to protect employees from unlawful firing.

Civility and Diversity

Modern compliance subjects include anti-bullying, anti-discrimination, and anti-harassment training, especially on the basis of gender, race, religion, age, nationality, or sexual orientation. Courses may apply these subjects generally across all relationships, or with a focus on hiring, vendor selection, management practices, team building, customer service, or any other area where a lack of inclusion and civility or the perception of prejudice poses a risk.

Responsible Stewardship

Modern compliance subjects include courses preventing the misuse or abuse of public or private resources and courses on specific environmental regulations, such as those in the automotive or utility industries. In many locations and industries, this category also includes courses on broader environmental concerns including sustainability, recycling, and waste reduction.

Fraud and Corruption

Modern compliance subjects include broad courses guarding against conflict of interest and nepotism, insider trading, bribery, price collusion, and improper gifts. In more regulated industries—such as finance, insurance, utilities, and college athletics—this category includes specific rules and protections designed to ensure fair market conditions within each industry. For example, this includes courses on Federal Energy Regulatory Commission (FERC) rules governing the fair sales and distribution of electricity to the grid, and courses on National Collegiate Athletic Association (NCAA) rules governing what is and is not allowed when recruiting a student athlete.

Data Privacy and Cyber Security

Modern compliance subjects include courses on the Health Insurance Portability and Accountability Act of 1996 (HIPAA) or the Family Educational Rights and Privacy Act (FERPA), which protect consumer privacy and ensure responsible safeguards for medical and educational records, respectively. More recently, this category has added broader courses on how to prevent and respond to cyber security threats, how to report system breaches, and how to safely handle PII (personally identifiable information) that may be collected from an organization's customers, affiliates, or employees.

Ethics and Integrity

Modern compliance subjects include courses on your organization's code of conduct or ethics policies, as well as broader courses supporting ethical decision-making among management, bystander intervention training, and anti-retaliation training that encourages employees to report and respond to unethical behavior.

These themes can be a useful tool for categorizing and consolidating our compliance training courses, as suggested in part 3 of this book, but they also speak to the higher-order values that compliance programs and policies are ultimately trying to serve. The goal of all compliance laws and policies is ultimately to create a more just and ethical environment for us all, usually in one of the seven ways shown here. By tracing individual courses and programs back to this shared foundation, we begin to see the real organizational value that good compliance learning can achieve.

This list also underscores the universality of our modern compliance training challenge. Whatever your industry or location, regardless of the specific laws and acronyms with which you are striving to comply, it's difficult to imagine an organization in the world today that wouldn't have risks and needs in each of these seven categories. Many organizations have chosen to manage those risks, at least in part, with mandatory employee training. And so the scope of compliance training only continues to expand.

Compliance at a Crossroads

We will discuss the traditional compliance program further in the following chapters, but it's worth noting here that it has served its function well. We've come a long way over the last century in advancing justice, safety, security, and fairness for our employees and citizens. That progress has been a result of carefully enacted laws like the Federal Sentencing Guidelines for Organizations, lawsuits that leverage those laws to win settlements and spark accountability, and organizations that have chosen to self-regulate in an effort to stave off future regulation and mitigate current legal risks.

These efforts should not be undersold. It is thanks largely to these reactive, legal pressures that worksites are so much safer than they were 50 years ago, that sexual and racial discrimination has been relegated further and further from hiring decisions and housing transactions, and that the Pentagon is no longer paying $600 for its toilet seats. These are just a few of the benefits that the traditional compliance program has ushered in, and for that we must all be grateful.

However, traditional compliance training may have reached its full potential. The low-hanging fruit has already been plucked, and the remaining challenges are more complex and varied than a simple policy or content-heavy tutorial can address. If we hope to continue our collective progress over the next 10, 50, or 100 years, we are going to need a new approach.

Our broader organizations are beginning to see that need, and so are our lawmakers, as the following examples illustrate.

In 2004, the Federal Sentencing Guidelines for Organizations was amended to specify that "check-the-box" compliance programs would not have a mitigating effect on organizational sentences. If organizations expected to be let off the hook for their employees' indiscretions, they had to show that their programs were designed to create "an organizational culture that encourages ethical conduct and a commitment to compliance with the law" (USSC 2004). This meant proper funding for response and prevention, proper analysis to undercover real areas of risk, and properly designed programs to reduce those risks through actual behavior change. In other words, it required an instructional designer's approach to compliance.

In 2017, the U.S. Department of Justice pressed further still in its Evaluation of Corporate Compliance Programs. The guidance underscored the vital importance of analyzing and remediating the root causes of misconduct, and championed best practices in training and communication to make sure those attempts at remediation stick. Among other considerations, the report emphasized that effective compliance programs should be able to answer questions like:

- "What analysis has the organization undertaken to determine who should be trained and on what subject?"
- "Has the training been offered in a form and language appropriate for the intended audience?"
- "Has the company measured the effectiveness of the training?" (USDJ n.d.).

In 2018, a joint task force of the United Kingdom, Mexico, Colombia, and Argentina took this focus on behavior even further. Created to stem corruption in the public sector, including costly corruption in the purchasing practices and quality of public school meals, the group began advocating for policies and programs that "focus on specific behaviors and their underlying motivators" to craft solutions that actually change those behaviors. As the *Wall Street Journal* noted in its article on the task force, "The U.K. government's move to add behavioral sciences research to its arsenal in the fight against corruption puts the country at the forefront of an emerging compliance landscape, one where understanding the drivers of human conduct is encouraged to counter the risk of mechanical, tick-the-box compliance practice" (Stein 2017).

Developments like these—and every new law that wisely requires "rigorous," "effective," or "measurable" training, instead of just training—should come as a massive relief to learning and development professionals. By promoting a renewed focus on prevention through real behavior change, regulatory agencies and our organizations' senior leaders are finally asking learning professionals to do the jobs we were hired to do, and we should be eager to rise to the challenge.

Hopefully, the next century of compliance will be remembered as the era of the learner. To hasten that progress, the majority of this book will prioritize the learner's needs and perspective, and detail how great learning can most effectively meet those needs to eliminate misconduct before it happens. But we must remember that we aren't starting from scratch. Our work is only possible because of the conscientious work of the women and men who have already dedicated their careers to compliance. These compliance subject matter experts (SMEs) were immersed in their subjects long before we arrived, and they will remain entrenched in their areas of expertise long after our learning projects are done.

Before we can convince our compliance SMEs what good training can do for our learners and our organizations, we need to assure them that these new, behavior-based efforts can still give them everything they need to meet their legal, risk-management requirements. And that buy-in can't be hesitant or half-hearted. If we are to succeed in fixing compliance training, we can't do it alone. We need the invested partnership of all our compliance stakeholders, especially the experts who ultimately own the risks.

So who are these SMEs, what do they want, and how can we convince them to give our learners what they need? Our ability to make great compliance training stick depends on the answers to those three questions, and they will be the focus of the next chapter.

Chapter 2
Who Owns Compliance?

If you hope to navigate your next compliance training project to a successful conclusion, you must be able to answer a fundamental question: Who is your primary stakeholder? Who sets the beat to which everyone else on the project must march? Who determines the bar against which the success of your final course will be measured?

Exhibit 2-1. Who Is Your Primary Stakeholder?

The primary stakeholder on most compliance training projects is _____ .	The training department supervisor
	The subject matter expert for the content
	The organization's learners
	The president or CEO of the organization
	The instructional designer

If you're having trouble answering the question in Exhibit 2-1, a simple thought experiment might help. Imagine you've built a beautiful new e-learning tutorial. You've invested nearly 200 development hours to create a best-in-class solution with slick video content, professional audio narration, and full captioning and accessibility. You've tested every interaction and proofread every line of text. You've adhered strictly to the project plan throughout, navigating your stakeholders through a number of review and update cycles, and tomorrow you're scheduled to implement the final product.

Now imagine you receive a phone call with some unwelcome news. All your hard work is about to be scrapped, at the eleventh hour, because one member of your project team is no longer satisfied with the approach. He'd like you to go back and add a slew of new content, including several whole new modules, and he'd like you to complete this laundry list of new changes as quickly as possible.

This lone person has just bloated your budget, dashed your deadline, and ransacked the flow of your meticulously structured course. In this thought experiment, who did you imagine that person to be?

It wasn't the instructional designer, who now has to work even harder to strap together some semblance of cohesion from all this new content. It likely wasn't the manager of the learning team either, who wouldn't want to jeopardize the project plan to amend content that had already been reviewed and approved by all stakeholders. It wasn't the learner either, who likely doesn't even know your course exists yet and who would surely prefer you cut content rather than add more. So, who made the call? Who has the authority to say what counts as right and wrong, and send everyone back to the drawing board?

If you've worked on more than one compliance training project in your career, you probably knew exactly who was on the other end of that call. On most compliance projects, this kind of change would only happen at the behest of the project's subject matter expert, or SME. And it happens all the time.

While the phrase *compliance training* implies a sharing of responsibility between compliance experts and learning and development professionals, the emphasis is almost always placed on the former. After teaching ATD's Compliance Essentials Course for the last three years, I've met countless beleaguered learning professionals who universally bemoan their lack of power to instigate change, even though they know change is needed to improve the quality and effectiveness of their training. These individuals—from organizations across multiple industries and countries—all confirm the same fundamental truth: by policy or practice, compliance SMEs usually assume full ownership and control of compliance training projects. For better or worse, they own compliance.

SMEs deem what content is required, and what is not. Their budgets foot the bill for development, and their signatures are the milestones that mark each deliverable. If we are to solve the problems that plague compliance training, we're going to have to learn to influence these key players and collaborate with them on a more even footing. But first, we need to give them what they want.

What SMEs Want

Depending on the compliance subject, the responsible SME for your next compliance project may sport one of many potential titles. You may find yourself working to appease a risk management officer, a lawyer or legal counsel, an auditor, or a specialist from a range of regulated areas like HR, finance, environmental health and safety, or IT, to name a few.

Whether or not this individual has taken the bar exam, modern compliance culture forces all compliance SMEs to think, at least a little, like lawyers. This legal focus expresses itself in a few recurring demands, which you'll likely see translated directly into most of the compliance courses and programs you've encountered at your organization.

The Universal Needs of the Compliance SME

Regardless of their field or industry, compliance subject matter experts are recognizable by their recurring demands, which can typically be traced back to a few core needs.

An Audit Trail

Whether courses are in-person or online, SMEs demand that the right participants are enrolled, that the rosters are dated and signed, and that your learning system reports can show definitively who took the course and when. They never know which participant may land the organization in legal trouble next, but if that happens, the participant's training records will be critically important to a potential legal defense. On your next compliance training project, don't be surprised if enrollment and reporting dominate your team's discussions.

Thorough Content

The legal system instills a strong desire for comprehensiveness among those responsible for compliance. For many SMEs, it's better to repeat messages or include irrelevant content than to cut a piece of content that ends up tied to the organization's next costly mistake. Learning professionals know that less is more for adult learners, but for compliance-driven SMEs, more might never be enough, and less is a frightening proposition.

Carefully Vetted Courses and Materials

One of the biggest problems plaguing compliance training is its propensity for simplified examples and dry legal jargon. Instead of considering our learner's language and lived experience, we're often asked to regurgitate canned language from previous courses or lift passages directly from the course policy or law. Real learning is most needed in the messy gray areas of real life, but SMEs often prefer cut-and-dried repetition, rather than risking a misinterpretation that could undo all their training investment.

Why SMEs Win

In an increasingly litigious environment, it's easy to see why the SME's three core needs have flourished. Legal risks are a real and pressing threat to our organizations, and training is a core pillar of our legal defense. That defense crumbles if training completion cannot be proven in court, if the subject of the litigated incident wasn't expressly covered, or if the language or structure of the learning includes too much nuance for a wily lawyer to exploit. The result is a strong desire for carefully vetted training that reads and feels like a contract.

According to a 2017 benchmarking study of compliance programs and officers by Navex Global, 41 percent of respondents had used evidence of their training programs to strengthen their defense in real legal cases (Fredeen 2017). These respondents noted, on average, "that their training programs had been used in a defense setting four times in the past three years." Our SMEs' frequent preoccupation with the legal ramifications of our training is not a sign of paranoia or an overabundance of caution. It's a rational response to a real and persistent threat.

However, by catering to these desires exclusively, we've built libraries of unwieldy, redundant, irrelevant compliance tutorials and courses that have earned our learners' disinterest, cynicism, and scorn. By turning training into a piece of legal evidence, we've created a body of corporate learning that works great for lawyers, but terribly for learners.

The legal focus of compliance training has dominated for so long that it may not be questioned by the stakeholders on your next compliance project. Compliance training is simply what modern organizations do to protect themselves from legal risk, one of the many costs of competing in a complex, modern economy. Even our learners are beginning to accept their compliance fate, learning how to multitask through annual training efforts to buy themselves another year of peace and quiet.

But just because we've all learned to hold our nose and take our medicine, there's no reason to believe it has to taste so bad. Luckily, there's a new group of compliance experts who are willing to rethink the prescription. They're ready to pick up the history of compliance where we left off in the last chapter—and take its future in a bold new direction.

Learning, Behavior, and the New SME

Parts 2 and 3 of this book are dedicated to tips, tools, and tricks to help you make the most of every compliance training opportunity, generating the kind of behavioral big wins that can fuel a satisfying compliance training career and add credibility to the learning and development profession. Unfortunately, that success is predicated on having an invested partner who sees the real value of behavioral compliance training and trusts you to do it right.

For compliance officers and experts at many organizations, training is nothing but another box to check in a long list of boxes, another nonnegotiable requirement to be met, another volley in a scattershot approach to mitigating risk as comprehensively as possible. Most of these compliance experts do not come from a learning background, and many view the learning function with no small degree of cynicism. Some may not even believe that people are capable of learning or changing. "If they were," these compliance experts think, "they wouldn't need me to police them."

Good subject matter experts and compliance officers, like those we met in Dallas at the opening of this book, are recoiling in repulsion at the paragraph above. They don't want to think of themselves as police officers or box-checkers, but as change agents and culture champions. These invested stakeholders will be vital to any effort to fix compliance training, but unfortunately they don't yet have a monopoly on their field. The world of compliance is changing rapidly, to be sure, but many organizations are still mired in a reactionary, heavy-handed past.

These less progressive experts are not bad or lazy people. They are simply playing the role that their organizations have asked them to serve, running the same compliance playbook that allowed their predecessors to protect their organizations for decades, and doing exactly what they believe they are expected to do.

For those still vested in a traditional mindset, the suggestions of this book will constitute a dramatic new approach to compliance. And change, as we all know, is scary. As dedicated learning professionals, if we wish to serve our full responsibility to our learners and our organizations, we must not only be great instructional designers, developers, and facilitators at companies like this—we must be outstanding agents of change.

We need to convince our most reluctant SMEs that we are just as interested in managing risk as they are. Then, with an eye toward learning and behavior, we can show them a better way.

Chapter 3
A Better Way to Manage Risk

A manager makes a racially insensitive remark during an interview. An employee is sexually harassed on the job. A customer's privacy is compromised. Mistakes and misconduct are a near constant in our lives. For recent evidence, look no further than Volkswagen, Uber, Wells Fargo, Harvey Weinstein, Google, Facebook and the litany of financial and civil indiscretions that keep the world's blogs and newspapers perennially full of bad news.

In a world where everyone is connected nearly all the time, even one-time mistakes can yield disastrous consequences. And as the cases above make clear, those consequences cannot be safely quarantined to an individual bad actor. Instead, in the most salacious cases, the public demands answers from a higher power. How, they ask, did the organization allow this to happen?

Depending on the scale of the offense and the degree of perceived negligence, organizations may face stock self-offs, trashed credit scores, consumer backlash, and forfeiture of grants or partnerships. In certain situations, complicit or negligent executives could be found personally liable, and may even find themselves behind bars. Simply claiming ignorance or proving that the bare minimum precautions were in place is no longer a viable defense. If the court of public opinion deems that a company could or should have done more to prevent misconduct, there will be costs to pay, in one form or another. In some recent cases, the organization never gets back to business as usual, forced to reckon forever with new market realities and an unending stream of consequences, all stemming from a single bad apple.

Luckily, thanks in large part to the federal sentencing guidelines discussed in chapter 1, the playbook for surviving the legal ramifications of these scandals is clear and readily available. Unfortunately, that playbook is doing little to actually prevent bad behavior. The rules of this approach have served our organizations well in the courtroom, but they have nearly eviscerated the trust of our learners and the public in the process.

Different Ways to Manage Risk

Imagine you were a compliance officer tasked with helping your organization avoid the potentially momentous legal costs associated with the inappropriate behaviors we discussed at the beginning of this chapter. Where would you start?

If you were looking to design a risk management strategy, you'd have three real options at your disposal:

- Meet your legally mandated training requirements and the precedent set by your peers, so that when misconduct inevitably occurs you can claim in court that you did all that was reasonably required to prohibit and discourage the behavior, thus avoiding collective responsibility and lessening any potential legal sentence levied on the organization.
- Deliver risk-specific training that shows your company takes its most pressing threats seriously and does everything it can to educate its employees in key areas of risk, thus reducing the likelihood of inappropriate behavior and improving your chances of a successful legal defense should the misconduct occur despite your good-faith efforts.
- Create a community of ethical decision-makers who exercise their own stellar judgment in every situation, thus eliminating entirely the kinds of mistakes that could land your organization in legal trouble.

Because the last option seems unobtainable, the first option has too often been the modern organization's only risk management strategy. Instead of actually trying to change people, we seem to have accepted that people will sometimes do bad things, no matter what, and we simply have to hope that those bad actors don't bring judgment on the rest of us. All we can do, we seem to think, is to tell everyone to act appropriately, and hope we won't be found complicit when they inevitably don't.

We've forgotten that there's a middle path. We might not be able to change everyone, that's true, but behavior does change. Behaviors change all around us, every day. And often, they change as a result of learning.

If we can follow the second path and focus on real needs, we can affect behavior. That means we can diminish the chance of misconduct, reduce our risk in absolute terms, and increase our likelihood of a sound legal defense if a determined bad actor refuses to see the light.

All we need to do to fix compliance training is to convince our stakeholders that the middle path is possible. We have to persuade our organizations that learning and development professionals are capable of changing people. We need to show them that there is a better way to handle risk management, and that we know the path.

To make that argument effectively, we first need to assuage our stakeholders' fears that our meddling might actually be exposing the organization to greater risk. That means we can't just be learning or behavior experts anymore. We must become risk management experts too.

The Traditional Compliance Program, As Seen at a Bowling Alley

Imagine you are the coach of an amateur bowling team. Your team is good and performs well in your weekend matches, but every now and then someone throws a gutter ball. You learn to hate these rare gutter balls; they are embarrassing, unsightly, and extremely costly. In fact, in your highly competitive league, a gutter ball in a single frame almost always leads to a loss for the entire team.

If you'll forgive the somewhat flippant analogy, these gutter balls are not unlike the costly corporate mistakes we've been discussing. A single case of apparent harassment, fraud, or negligence can jeopardize a year or more of good corporate planning, just as a single misguided roll of the ball can cost your team the game. If we extend the analogy further, we can begin to see why traditional compliance programs have a training problem, and how a new approach to risk can solve it.

Putting yourself back in the shoes of our bowling coach, how would you address the issue of these occasional gutter balls? If the bowling alley was run like a traditional compliance program, you might be surprised at how little your response would focus on the actual act of bowling. To understand why, we need to explore how this unusual bowling alley keeps score.

A gutter ball is bad in this strange league, obviously much worse than a strike, but it's only really harmful if a group of regulatory agencies and legal professionals deem you, the coach, to be complicit in the gutter ball or negligent in its prevention. Much like the Federal Sentencing Guidelines for Organizations that we discussed in the previous chapter, the league can choose to hold the entire team responsible for gutter balls that occur on your watch, or they can hold the individual bowler accountable and let the rest of you off the hook with a slap on the wrist. Their decision depends, primarily, on the balance of mitigating and aggravating factors they find for your team, as defined in their gutter ball sentencing guidelines. Simply put, you can avoid collective responsibility if you can prove that you and your team took reasonable steps to discourage and respond to the gutter ball.

Getting off the hook for gutter balls, it turns out, is far easier than avoiding them all together. The league has graciously documented the precautions they deem reasonable, and all you have to do is follow their playbook to effectively manage your risk and reduce the likelihood that your team could be found complicit should a gutter ball occur.

If your bowling league employed the seven pillars of the traditional compliance program we discussed in chapter 1, which still dictate the full compliance landscape at many organizations, these reasonable precautions would include the following elements.

Policies and Standards

You must write and post a gutter ball policy for your bowlers, clearly defining what a gutter ball is, why it is unacceptable, and how it will be disciplined if it occurs on your team. All your bowlers must read and attest their understanding to the gutter ball policy at the beginning of each season, and a copy of the policy must be available at the alley for their continuous review.

Executive Leadership

You, as team coach, must take an active interest in gutter ball prevention. You should be vigilant in monitoring for potential gutter balls and continuously demonstrate your commitment to keeping each roll squarely on the lane. If your other responsibilities do not allow the time and attention required for effective monitoring and enforcement, you can delegate a gutter ball officer to manage your gutter ball program at an executive level.

Reporting Channels

You must ensure that all team members are able and encouraged to report any known or suspected gutter balls in a timely manner. These reports should be welcomed and quickly escalated to the appropriate members of your leadership team, without any fear of retaliation.

Monitoring and Audits

Your team must conduct routine audits to report on the overall health of your gutter ball prevention program. This may include metrics that track your total gutter ball events year over year, analytics to shine light on any trends of heightened gutter ball risk, and team surveys that reveal the strength of your program in creating a genuine anti-gutter ball culture.

Incentives and Performance Management

You should further demonstrate your commitment to avoiding gutter balls by ensuring that good bowlers are recognized and rewarded for doing what's right, while those who roll gutter balls are consistently penalized in accordance with your policies, regardless of their role or popularity within your organization. If you are serious about gutter balls, they should be baked into the foundation of your performance management programs, with gutter ball prevention competencies factored into raises, promotions, and other personnel decisions.

Training and Communication

You should have a robust training and communications plan to ensure that all your bowlers are informed about the nuances of your gutter ball prevention program, including a detailed look at the league guidelines that gave rise to your program and the full policies and standards you've implemented to meet those guidelines. This training should be mandatory and regularly refreshed, likely executed through an hour-long gutter ball e-learning tutorial your entire team will be required to take each year. Just to be safe, nonbowlers working in or near the alley should also be required to take the training.

Response and Prevention

You should respond quickly and effectively in the event of a gutter ball, making every effort to alert the public and notify the appropriate league officials before the impact of the gutter ball can spread. Following a thorough investigation of the incident, you should identify the factors that allowed the gutter ball to occur and do whatever you can to reduce the chance of a similar incident in the future. For example, you could remove the gutter ball bowler from your team.

* * *

While different organizations and compliance writers may label or re-organize these pillars in a number of different ways, the standard list shown here illustrates the two unspoken assumptions that drive traditional compliance training and the broader compliance programs in which they exist:

- Bad actors choose to engage in bad behavior.
- Bad behavior is inevitable.

To be fair, the thoughtful SMEs and compliance officers interviewed for this book would never claim these assumptions as their own. In fact, many feel called to the work precisely because they hope to improve safety, security, and social justice in their communities. Some compliance professionals might indulge the first assumption, at least in private, but few would be willing to call misconduct inevitable. Their job, after all, is to prevent misconduct, and you can't very well sell yourself as a prevention specialist for the inevitable.

And yet, these two assumptions are what our learners see when they look beneath the tone and content of our traditional compliance programs.

Why else would the seven pillars of the traditional compliance program have thrived for so long? Why else would the pillars of training and prevention be interpreted so narrowly, relegated to mere afterthoughts at the end of the list, instead of driving our compliance efforts as this book will ultimately suggest they should? The answer, whether we acknowledge it or not, is that we don't really believe we have another option.

If we believe that certain people and roles are prone to misconduct, and that their decisions are willful and impossible to prevent, then we are all going to find ourselves in court eventually. And when we find ourselves on trial for that next inevitable mistake, our only chance of success is to convince the court of those very same assumptions. The mistake is regrettable, we'll argue, but due entirely to the unfortunate and unpreventable decisions of a bad actor. The individual crime is punished, fairly, and the organization lives to profit another day.

The seven pillars of the traditional compliance program are fantastic at winning this kind of case, allowing us to confidently say, "We told them not to. We showed them we were serious time and again. We reacted as responsibly as we could to keep it from happening again."

If we can make those claims convincingly, with evidence that all seven pillars were in place, the traditional compliance program wins our exoneration.

This approach works because these assumptions—that selfish, ignorant, or short-sighted people will do bad things from time to time, and that we can't really stop them—have permeated the legal system through decades of case precedent and seminal documents like the Criminal Sentencing Guidelines. The clear but unspoken message from our governments and regulatory agencies has almost always been: "We expect you to take every reasonable precaution to keep this kind of thing from happening, but we know it will happen sometimes, and we'll work with you when it does."

Given the long, slow history of compliance that we explored in chapter 1, this approach is understandable and appropriate. Only a century ago, organizations were entirely unwilling and unequipped to safeguard their customers, protect their employees, or preserve the fairness of the markets in which they would compete. By striking a reasonable balance between aspirations and reality, our laws and regulations have helped us enjoy a century of progress without too much social or economic disruption along the way. However, in large part because of that progress, "good enough" might not be good enough anymore.

A Harsher Jury

Arguing "we told them not too" might once have been enough to satisfy a traditional judge using a traditional interpretation of the Criminal Sentencing Guidelines, especially if you could provide ample evidence to show that you took that message seriously. But this old argument isn't likely to appease the new seat of justice in the compliance world: the public. Whether it is fair to be judged by the sometimes fickle, occasionally ill-informed whims of the masses is debatable, but that debate isn't likely to restore stock prices or save a beleaguered CEO once the public has made up its mind.

A confluence of factors are dramatically changing expectations—including rising standards of fairness and corporate responsibility, rising doubt in the intentions of our business and political leaders to meet those standards, and rising faith in the infallibility of money and technology to solve virtually any problem an organization genuinely wants to solve. These factors have nearly eliminated concepts like "good-faith effort" and the "benefit of the doubt" from all proceedings in the court of public opinion. If you are a CEO and a highly visible mistake happens on your watch, this new court either finds that you wanted it to happen, or that you didn't care enough to stop it. A policy, a firing, and a few training records aren't likely to convince this harsh court otherwise.

Even more frightening to the modern CEO is the scale of punishment the public can administer. Forget fines and probationary periods; a guilty verdict in the court of public opinion can generate massive stock sell-offs, customer boycotts, and a permanent hit to your marketing power. Perhaps it's no surprise, given the severity of these risks, that recent indiscretions have led to dramatic changes in senior leadership, even at large, successful organizations. Our CEOs have more skin in the game than ever before. And they are taking notice.

Also taking note are the politicians and regulatory agencies who traditionally shape and assess our compliance programs. Responding to the public mood, these agencies are beginning to shift their expectations too, asking for more proven prevention practices than simply establishing policies and reacting when those policies are broken. There are a number of new laws that have moved beyond mere training requirements that can be satisfied with "training for the sake of training" approaches. Title IX is a great example, with subsequent guidance from the U.S. Department of Education demanding not just training, but effective, measurable, pedagogically sound training. That is a high bar for many organizations to hit, and it will likely continue rising with each new costly headline.

All this change is causing no shortage of heartburn for traditional compliance officers, executives, and SMEs. Given the two unspoken assumptions we've already discussed—that bad people do bad things and there's little we can do to stop a determined bad actor—it's fair for these individuals to wonder if they are being set up to fail. Luckily for both hard-working compliance professionals and our species at large, those two assumptions are only half the story of human behavior.

A Higher Standard for Human Behavior

The truth is, the public is right. Our organizations can solve almost any problem we truly wish to solve, even complex behavioral issues that seem unpredictable and unavoidable in the moment. We simply have to dedicate the time and resources to understanding the factors that influence those actions, and then use learning and performance solutions to change how people interpret and react to those factors in the future.

Embracing this new approach requires two new compliance assumptions:

- Bad decisions are not always inevitable.
- People behave in predicable ways, primarily in response to their situation.

In other words, we can follow the middle path outlined at the beginning of this chapter. We may not be able to prevent every incident of misconduct every time, but we can take tangible steps that make incidents less frequent and less harmful. Things happen for a reason, and if we can understand those reasons, we can make a difference.

These new assumptions don't negate the traditional assumptions we've already made. CEOs, salespeople, accountants, managers, and everyday employees may still occasionally do bad things, either out of selfishness, ignorance, or a badly prioritized set of values. Sometimes the behavior is perpetrated by a single individual over an entire lifetime, as in the Harvey Weinstein scandal, and sometimes it's a symptom of a broken culture that deliberately cultivates dangerous priorities through every level of the organization, as in the well-documented case of nefarious sales practices at Wells Fargo.

The best an ethics or compliance officer can do in these situations is to notice the bad actions quickly and respond. Training likely won't fix the internally motivated misconduct illustrated in these examples, that much is true. But these cases only account for one portion of our compliance risk, and they are already addressed by the traditional compliance program pillars in place at most organizations. If a person or group willingly violates a written policy that has been consistently enforced and communicated, it will be simple enough to remove those individuals from your organization and survive any legal challenges that may ensue.

But if we want to raise our chances of success in the stickier cases—the more common gray areas where our corporate responsibility is truly up for debate—we should shift our attention away from just catching and penalizing bad actors. Instead, we need to focus on creating learning that can help the majority of well-intentioned people in our audience who sometimes do bad things.

These people do not wake up in the morning intent on ignoring the law and behaving unethically. Their actions aren't due to ignorance of our expectations or a willing desire to subvert our policies. Instead, their mistakes are the result of competing priorities, inadequate skills, and situational influences; problems that training can very gamely attempt to solve.

For an example, let's return our attention to our beleaguered bowling team. Assuming each team member possesses an average bowler's mindset, the traditional compliance pillars would do nothing to change their likelihood of success or failure. They already know gutter balls are bad, and they already know the consequences to the team could be serious. The policies and training required by the bowling league have little real impact on the bowlers themselves, except to waste their time. The bowlers don't want to throw a gutter ball in the first place, and if they could avoid it, they certainly would. That brings us to the good news for both of you: Gutter balls, like many behavioral mistakes, are perfectly avoidable.

Perhaps, instead of a dry training tutorial that focuses on policies and procedures, you should analyze your team to find their real needs and craft learning solutions that actually make them better bowlers. This may mean correcting one team member's footwork or adjusting the ball weight for another. Perhaps you realize that formal training isn't right for your audience at all. Instead, you could partner your best bowlers with your worst bowlers for private mentoring games, giving those who are struggling a chance to learn informally and without consequence from others who have mastered the ropes.

Or perhaps you discover in your analysis that there isn't a talent problem at all. Maybe the lanes are too slick or too dry, and you could talk to the bowling alley staff about creating more conducive conditions. Or maybe you could go all-in on prevention, investing in a set of gutter bumpers to guarantee all future throws stay firmly on the lane.

The right answer for your situation depends on the severity and prevalence of the risk, the constraints of your industry and organization, and the needs of your learners. By taking the question of behavior change seriously, you not only lower the likelihood of empty frames in your future, you also improve the quality of your legal defense if an unfortunate gutter ball slips through the cracks. Should that day ever come, you can stand before a judge or the court of public opinion and confidently say: "We took this risk seriously, we went above and beyond in our efforts to understand it and prevent it, and we'll do everything we can to keep it from happening again." With evidence of a robust, behavior-centered learning plan—along with the other compliance program pillars we've already discussed—you'll be more likely to win a legal argument than you would have been with a traditional compliance program. Even more important, your new program will actually reduce the risk of misconduct by changing behavior, which makes you less likely to appear in court, or the far tougher court of public opinion, in the first place.

To achieve these twin benefits of improved prevention and mitigation, we simply need to reorder our approach to the traditional compliance pillars. Components like policies, executive buy-in, and auditing still matter, but they should complement our programs, not drive them. If we want to build compliance programs that make a real difference, we have to put learning and prevention in front of the parade.

Leading the Parade

"We spend too much time sweeping up behind messes that have already happened," said Earnie Broughton, senior advisor with the Ethics and Compliance Initiative, during an interview for this book. "If we really want to make a difference, we have to be leading the parade."

Broughton sees this shift happening through a renewed focus on the sources of human behavior, as he explains in part 2. His desire to "lead the parade" is a compelling and succinct call to action for trainers, risk management officers, auditors, lawyers, and everyone else with a stake in organizational compliance. We can be doing more than sweeping up messes; we can lead our organizations down a better path.

On its surface, this may not sound like a revolutionary concept. Organizations invest in compliance and risk management teams because they genuinely want to prevent and mitigate risk. Whether motivated by a fundamental regard for the well-being of the world around them, or a cynical calculation of how costly that well-being can be to repair, executives at the highest level are starting to demand real effectiveness from our compliance programs.

And yet, a box-checking mentality still permeates the tone and construction of most compliance training efforts, as you can quickly confirm with the following simple experiment:

1. Find an employee who has worked at your organization for at least 10 years. This individual should have been a required learner for some or all of your compliance training efforts, but without any stake in shaping those efforts. In other words, the employee should represent an average member of your learning audience.

2. Ask this employee why your compliance training courses and programs exist. What purpose do they believe those courses were designed to serve?

3. Time how long it takes for this individual to utter the phrase, "checking a box."

You can gauge the scope of your compliance learning problem by how quickly box-checking is evoked by your learners. If it tends to be the first line of their response, you're reading this book at a good time.

This disconnect between our intentions and our audience's perception may be unsettling, but it's hardly surprising given the facts we've explored so far. While the scope of our modern compliance burden has continued to grow, the focus of our compliance training programs has remained set on risk mitigation instead of risk reduction. As a result, all our incentives are compelling us away from meaningful, learner-focused learning, and toward delivering compressive overviews of as many laws, policies, and potential mistakes as we can, all forced as often as possible on as many employees as possible. This approach has raised our odds of success in mitigating legal sentences, as supporting by the Federal Sentencing Guidelines for Organizations, but it has done little to change behavior. Instead, it has created the valid and dangerous perception from our learners that we are only interested in checking boxes.

It's time for something better. Compliance officers and executives want to quit sweeping up after the parade and start leading it in the right direction.

As learning and development professionals, we are uniquely suited to help with that transition.

We are our organization's resident experts in behavior change, and we know the learning principles that can make a difference. We can analyze our audience's needs and equip them with the skills and knowledge that allow them to not just refrain from bad behavior, but to thrive within their legal and ethical constraints. We can make an organization a better place to work and improve its bottom line, all through real learning.

These may seem like bold claims, but they are well within reach. We simply need to reorder our traditional compliance approach and start looking at our compliance training through a behavioral, learner-centered lens. Given current legal and societal trends, it is only a matter of time before your organization is ready to make that transition. And when they come to you, the learning team, for help, you must be ready to speak on behalf of your learners.

PART 2:
THE
LEARNERS

Chapter 4
The Rise of Real Learning

If you were listening to NPR on your drive home from work on November 8, 2017, you may have heard an alarming call to action for U.S. learning professionals. The main story during that evening's commute featured employment lawyers, a slew of recent case studies, and a summary of a 2016 report on sexual harassment prevention by the Equal Employment Opportunity Commission (EEOC). The piece convincingly reinforced the EEOC taskforce conclusion that "the last three decades of sexual harassment training haven't worked" (Noguchi 2017).

This is a harsh criticism on the value of traditional compliance training, but there's not much our industry can say to object. None of the lawyers interviewed for the segment could offer any evidence that any sexual harassment training had ever successfully changed behavior, despite the persistence and ubiquity of such programs in the corporate world for decades. The EEOC, in a subsequent summary of the report's findings, suggested it was time for a total reboot of the way our organizations address harassment prevention. "In the simplest terms," EEOC Commissioner Victoria A. Lipnic explained, "training must change."

Unfortunately, at many organizations, news stories like this may not come as much of a surprise. Many learners—and many trainers, for that matter—already know that compliance training as it has been traditionally interpreted is doing little to move the needle toward real behavior change. As this vague sense of dissatisfaction with training has grown, and as more lawyers and executives have begun to suspect that something isn't quite right in the world of learning and development, a number of troubling myths have emerged to explain our continued failure.

Perhaps, as the voices coming from my car's radio ventured, the problem with training is its format. "It doesn't help," said Patricia Wise, an employment lawyer and member of the EEOC taskforce that created the report, "that most online training courses are stilted and not engaging."

Broken Medium or Broken Message?

Sharing a view of many other executives and learning professionals, Wise used her NPR appearance to lament the shift away from in-person courses and toward online tutorials. "Employees really can zone out and not even pay attention to the training," she explained, echoing a common condemnation of e-learning programs.

It's true that budget cuts and the growing scope of compliance have sparked many organizations to move their training online, and that many senior decision makers are motivated by efficiency and cost more than e-learning's potential learning impact. As a result, e-learning is often seen by our leaders and learners as yet another piece in a long string of unfortunate but necessary compromises demanded by the modern world, generating all the cynicism and distrust that such compromises inevitably incur.

But all this distaste has little to do with the promise or potential of the medium itself. Online learning tools can support learners in totally new and exciting ways, and academic studies have found time and again that e-learning is an effective educational tool when employed in the right ways, for the right learners, toward the right purposes. Instead of a fair commentary on the format and its limitations, the collective disdain for online tutorials is likely only a result of the flawed messages they have been given to deliver. In this light, the current unpopularity of e-learning is just another symptom of our broken approach to compliance training, and another example of how that approach may be jeopardizing the long-term health of the entire learning and development industry.

Does Learning Ever Really Matter?

The learning and development industry is also threatened, existentially, by some even more troubling myths that our long-ineffectual compliance training has fostered: A growing cynicism toward learning and development as a field capable of achieving any real results, and the dangerous but seductive idea that people may not be capable of change.

Training can work for some limited skills and behaviors, these doubters may concede, but not for issues like ethical leadership, responsible conduct, or sexual harassment. You either are a harasser, or you aren't, and a training tutorial isn't going to change that. EEOC trailblazer Elaine Herskowitz offered this very view a little later in the aforementioned NPR segment, which obviously kept me sitting in my driveway until its conclusion. When asked if better training could stop more sexual harassment incidents, she replied, "I'm sorry, you just have to know that you cannot grab another person and kiss them without their consent."

This is a compelling articulation of a truth that many learning professionals already know from firsthand experience: Training is not the best solution to every problem. Some bad actors simply need to be removed from an organization before their damage can spread. Some behaviors need to be better incentivized or better disciplined if we expect change to stick. Some mistakes are better to correct by an engaged manager in the moment of need than to preempt across an entire organization by some canned training program encountered months, years, or decades before the mistake is likely to occur.

Many problems aren't due to a lack of skills or knowledge, and many behaviors can't be changed with a classroom session or online tutorial.

This argument certainly has some merit. There is a time and place for training, and a single course or tutorial is seldom a magic bullet. But if we take this notion too far, we risk underselling the real value that the learning function can and should be delivering to our organizations.

In reality, there is a simple explanation for why most traditional compliance training has failed to change behavior. After reading the opening chapters of this book, that explanation should be readily apparent. It does not fail because people are incapable of change or because e-learning tutorials are impossible to learn from. Compliance training fails to change behavior because it is rarely designed with real learning as its goal.

Learning for Learners

While it's true that learning and development may not be able to solve every compliance problem on its own, it remains one of the few available tools that any organization has to influence its employees' behavior. If we are going to achieve our organizational goals and our compliance mandates, we are going to need good training to play a role.

Not even the authors of that 2016 EEOC report on harassment prevention—the report that gave rise to the NPR segment—would claim that training can or should be discarded, despite its lack of a winning track record.

"We are not suggesting that training be thrown out; far from it," said Commissioner Lipnic in a subsequent summary on the EEOC website. Instead, she explained, "Training needs to be part of a holistic, committed effort to combat harassment, focused on the specific culture and needs of a particular workplace" (EEOC 2016).

A more holistic approach is certainly required, and if we truly hope to change behavior, training can't just go along for the ride. If we want to move the needle on mission-critical subjects like harassment, workplace safety, cyber security, corporate responsibility, and ethical decision making, we need to put learning at the heart of all our compliance efforts.

Instead of merely considering how another online tutorial can accommodate the needs of another compliance program or mandate, we need to explore how our compliance programs and mandates can start accommodating the real needs of our learners. We need a learning-centered approach to compliance.

How Learning Can Create Change

To better demonstrate the distinction between meaningful learning designed to make a difference and traditional tutorials designed only to comply, let's linger a little longer on the example of sexual harassment.

While gray-area cases and "sins of ignorance" may pose an important problem in some organizations, a significant portion of sexual harassment cases are perpetrated by serial predators who enjoy exploiting power dynamics and wielding control over others. While a good leader or learning professional may like to believe that no one is beyond improvement, it seems doubtful that an online training tutorial could make any progress in converting the hearts and minds of such callous harassers. The behavior of these predators isn't due to a lack of skills or knowledge, but to a character flaw that they have spent a lifetime developing. Training can't directly change their intentions, at least not on its own, but it can help mitigate or avoid their destructive actions by changing the behaviors of those around them. With a laser-like focus on the people and skills that it can hope to affect, training becomes a key prong in a harassment prevention approach that actually works to prevent harassment!

We only have to quit pretending that a training tutorial telling employees not to harass was ever a magic pill that could stop harassment in its tracks. "Seriously," these old tutorials seem to say, with a virtual wagging finger, "quit harassing." Our worst employees simply ignore the message or fail to see how it applies to them, while our best employees feel insulted by the exercise and annoyed that we're wasting their time on an ineffectual solution to a real problem. Or, they may not even realize the problem exists at their organization, and no one likes investing time or money in a solution to a nonproblem.

If we want to acknowledge real problems and elicit real change, we have to take a broader view of the corporate ecosystem in which harassing behavior occurs, and then target relevant points in that system where training can realistically make an impact.

Instead of hosting annual tutorials that spout legal definitions and tell average employees to refrain from egregious forms of sexual harassment most would never dream of committing—resulting in a "preach-to-the-choir" course that many people tune out, and your real predators and harassers would never learn from anyway—you could target specific learning components at specific audiences as part of a holistic learning plan. If you craft that plan with a steadfast aim to make the largest possible impact on behavior, given the real needs of your organization, you have a great chance of success.

As an analogy, consider a farmer locked in a losing battle with a persistent pest. No pesticides have succeeded in thwarting the pest itself, which continues to succeed in its steadfast intention of destroying the farmer's crops. Instead of continuing this losing head-on attack, the farmer turns her attention to the environment in which her assailant has thrived. Perhaps a change in the planting schedule could make conditions less hospitable for the pest. A small shift in the planting or harvesting process could render the pest's habitual behaviors impossible, forcing it to change its ways, perish, or move on to someone else's field.

With the trial-and-error approach of a dogged scientist, a good farmer would eventually succeed in eliminating the pest by changing the right combination of conditions around it. Similarly, in a good harassment prevention training plan, you could prevent the damaging behavior of even your most persistent harassers using strategic learning solutions that alter the environment in which such behavior occurs.

For example, you may elect to focus on bystander intervention training to help the silent majority of ethical, responsible employees take an active role in addressing inappropriate behavior and shaping a more civil environment. Or, you may find that your organization benefits more from reporting and nonretaliation training to ensure those being harassed are prepared to speak up quickly. Executive training may be useful to help ensure that your leadership is prepared to respond appropriately to those reports. Or you may wish to invest in civility training to help your colleagues empathize with one another and recognize how their inappropriate behavior may be perceived, ideally helping employees refrain from milder, unintentional forms of harassment before their misconduct evolves into a case that leaves you no choice but formal discipline.

These are just a few of the solutions that could have a measurable impact, even on a seemingly entrenched behavior like sexual harassment. The sidebar presents a more extensive toolbox of potential learning solutions, but even that list is not exhaustive. Depending on the specific needs of your organization and your audience, a successful approach may employ some or all these activities, as well as activities not listed that may offer the precise piece of support your audience is desperately waiting for.

Potential Toolbox for Strategic Learning Solutions

Instead of creating an anti-harassment training program centered on obvious rules and legal definitions, a program of strategic learning solutions can create real change by targeting the specific behaviors where it can have the greatest impact.

Bystander Intervention Training

Empower conscientious employees—who hopefully comprise the majority of your organization—to speak up and seek help when they witness harassment.

Organizational Self-Defense Training

Ensure that potentially vulnerable employee populations know their full legal and policy protections, and equip these individuals with specific reporting and feedback skills to ensure they can confidently stand up for those rights or seek help when needed.

Executive Response Training

Help your executives understand the human and legal costs if they fail to adequately respond to harassment, and provide an opportunity to practice crisis management in a safe setting before lives and corporate reputations are on the line.

Talent Acquisition Training

Prepare mid-level managers to spot signs of potential harassers early in the hiring process, and add selection criteria that awards candidates for qualities like empathy, compassion, and vigilance in the protection of their co-workers' rights. In male-dominated industries, the training could even be used to educate managers on the value of a diverse workforce and the importance of seeking out strong female candidates for open positions.

Performance Management Training

Similar to hiring discussions, equip your managers to include considerations like civility, empathy, and ethical action in their performance review process, allowing your organization to draw a tighter correlation between its stated values and the behaviors it rewards with promotion or financial gain.

Civility Training

If your training must target the entire organization at once, you may illicit more change by focusing on broader civility courses that emphasize values like compassion and kindness, which naturally lead to lower levels of harassment, instead of dwelling on specific types of harassment that can cause members of your organization to tune out or feel villainized. This kind of values-based training was specifically recommended by the EEOC report we discussed at the beginning of this chapter, as it has been shown to generate a more positive reaction from learners and evade some of the evils that can ensue when learners view compliance programs as corporate self-defense.

With educated guesses, a scientific approach, and a sound instructional design methodology, you can uncover the real causes of your organization's most pressing issues and create a program that produces a measurable difference.

How Learning Professionals Will Fix Compliance Training

We don't need to discard the sophisticated programs of compliance SMEs to reap the rewards of real learning, while continuing to benefit from the proven risk-management value that those programs afford. Instead, we simply need to ensure that the training components within those compliance programs are curated and controlled by learning professionals, and that every new compliance training solution we create is prioritized for its impact on our learners.

Whether you are implementing a full compliance learning plan or trying to make a single course as efficient and effective as possible within your current constraints, there are tangible tips and tools that can help you maximize relevancy, engagement, and impact in every stage of the training project life cycle. The remaining chapters in part 2 explore the most useful of these tips, presented in the order encountered during an average project:

- **Analyzing learners and content to reveal relevant needs.** To begin, we will focus on the most fundamental requirement of any effective learning project: a thorough understanding of your audience, their perspective on the subject, and their behavioral needs. Chapter 5 offers tips for completing learner-centered analysis within the constraints of any compliance subject.

- **Designing effective, behavioral solutions.** With your learners' needs thoroughly understood, you can begin to explore the best way to meet those needs in a real and lasting way. To succeed, you may need to think outside the traditional training box. In chapter 6, research from psychology and behavioral economics will help you envision solutions that go beyond mere training to find the right behavioral nudges that maximize the likelihood of change.

- **Developing compliance training solutions that stick.** Whether you are building an entirely new program or revising an existing tutorial, your success in transferring your learning objectives into action will depend on your ability to alter your learners' context, habits, or motivation. Chapters 7-9 will help you create great learning experiences by focusing on universal techniques like storytelling, problem-based learning, and cue-routine-reward cycles.

- **Implementing and evaluating compliance training to maximize its impact.** Once you've built your masterpiece, you need to ensure it's launched in a way that maximizes its appeal and longevity. Employees have spent years learning to be skeptical of compliance training—if you want your organization to benefit from your new approach, you need to brand and measure your offerings in a way that wins back their trust. Chapter 10 shows you how.

To begin, we will turn our attention to a critically important tool—the Compliance Training Analysis Form—and explore how opportunistic analysis can foster compliance training that feels real and relevant for your learners, because it *is* real and relevant.

Chapter 5

Opportunistic Analysis

Imagine you are a surgeon in a busy hospital. One afternoon, a patient storms into your office with an unmistakable air of urgency. "Doctor," he cries, "I need you to take out my appendix, right away."

What would you say? If you follow the customer-is-always-right mentality that governs many interactions between learning professionals and our compliance SMEs, you may already be reaching for your scalpel.

The need seems urgent, after all, and the customer obviously has a clear idea of what he wants. Leaving the analogy briefly for the real world, you may have SMEs come to you with entirely finished PowerPoint decks, asking you only to add some timed animations or narration and put it into your LMS. Building such a tutorial is a fairly simple job—just as removing an appendix would be for a skilled surgeon—and the easiest response is to simply give the customer what they want and get them out of your office. Another need successfully served, another appendix successfully removed, another tutorial successfully foisted on your employees.

However, by simply serving the stated needs of the SME without question, you've done little to actually help them, and even less to help your learners. As in our example, acting without any additional analysis is limited and reactionary at best, and dangerously negligent at worst.

Your learning expertise may not be welcome on every project by every SME, but you owe it to your organization and your learners to try. This means you may occasionally need to say no to the most egregious wastes of your learners' time, and that you must always ask the right questions to try to determine what learning can do to contribute to a solution.

Like a surgeon asking a few follow-up questions before putting a patient under for an operation, your dialogue with the SME should not be seen as difficult, contrarian, obstructionist, or challenging to their authority. If you handle the conversations correctly, stakeholders should leave your office feeling supported, understood, and better off than when they arrived. The key is not to say no to everything or to challenge indiscriminately—but only to make time for analysis.

With the right approach to analysis, you can ensure that you are making the most of every compliance training opportunity, that your legal obligations are satisfied, and that you're truly doing all you can for your SMEs, your learners, and the broader organization. Without such analysis, you may find yourself removing an appendix in an effort to resolve a headache.

Introducing the Compliance Training Analysis Form

As the title of this chapter suggests, the analysis phase of a compliance learning project requires a special brand of opportunism. To thrive within the constraints of a compliance subject, you must be able to identify and exploit the real behavioral opportunities within. In other words, you have to do more than just comply, while also ensuring you don't do anything less.

This is a fairly easy balance to strike once you get into the habit, and the Compliance Training Analysis Form, provided in appendix 1, is designed to help.

This two-page form is carefully structured to generate the precise balance required for deliverables that are both effective and compliant. By completing both pages with your project team at the beginning of each compliance training project, you can rest assured that your final product will balance the needs of all your stakeholders, including the most important and most often neglected: the learners.

Page 1: Identify Your Constraints

Constraints exist in any business environment, but they can be especially vexing on compliance projects. The training team can be saddled with a boatload of cumbersome constraints; most are fixed by an omnipotent external force, and many come in the form of one-size-fits-all regulations that somehow don't seem to fit anyone.

Such constraints can challenge the relevance and applicability of any learning initiative, and they can become a serious obstacle if they are accepted blindly. Unfortunately, blind implementation happens far too often. In the flawed reality of traditional compliance training, the course or tutorial becomes a mere summation of a subject's constraints and nothing more.

To fix compliance training, we need to quit thinking of a compliance subject's mandates as the outline of what its training must be. Instead, these constraints should be seen as a border. Our courses or tutorials must stay within those borders to ensure our core responsibilities are met, but we are free to draw whatever shape we'd like inside.

These constraints should not drive the final course any more than a frame should dictate the painting that is created within it—but that is not to say borders don't matter, or that legal requirements are unimportant. If the minimum mandates are not observed, your organization may face direct fines or regulatory consequences, or expose itself to legal risk by forfeiting the mitigating factors that traditional compliance training can provide in a courtroom. Legal requirements obviously matter and the first page of the Compliance Training Analysis Form is designed to establish a clear map of the specific legal or policy borders that exist so you can keep your design inside that frame.

By completing this page of the form with the appropriate SMEs at the beginning of each compliance training project, you can give the SME a voice in the process and establish a full list of boxes that the final learning offering must check.

Depending on the subject, the level of detail on page 1 can vary dramatically. Many laws and policies simply require "annual training for all employees," without any further stipulations on what that training must include. Such mandates show trust in the organization to build a training solution that works for its audience, providing the ultimate blank slate on which a good instructional designer can paint a behavioral learning masterpiece.

Other policies and laws, however, define what should count as training, and may stipulate countless hoops through which the final training deliverable must jump. Examples of specific training constraints may include:

- Specific hour requirements—"All managers must receive at least two hours of sexual harassment training each year."
- Specific definitions—"Training must include your state's current legal definition of consent."
- Specific responsibilities—"Training must inform mandatory reporters within your organization of their reporting responsibilities."
- Specific processes—"Training must show all employees how to report issues of sexual abuse or child endangerment."

Objectives like these—captured on page 1 of the Compliance Training Analysis Form—detail the constraints that your course must fit within. If such specific stipulations exist for a given compliance subject, it's critically important that your instructional designer and the entire project team know those constraints at the very beginning of the project. Whether the requirements are loosely bound or tightly defined should be irrelevant to the final deliverable's quality and impact, but the difference is critically important to the way the deliverables are structured, developed, and implemented. The frame should not define the learning experience, but it will undoubtedly affect it.

Once you know what your frame looks like, you may be wondering what should go inside. For that, we turn our attention to page 2 of our form.

Page 2: Identify Your Opportunities

If the first page of the Compliance Analysis Form is for the lawyers and SMEs, the second page is the land of the learner. With the letter of the law now clearly defined, the second page allows you to explore and serve its spirit.

This is your opportunity to align your training project with your organization's mission and your learners' actual needs, leaving you with a final compliance product that does much more than just comply. At this stage, the form allows the project team to consider:

- What are the most pressing risks to our organization in this category?
  - Where are we squandering the greatest potential value?

- Which forms of misconduct or neglect could be most disastrous to our customers, our employees, or our bottom line?
- Which risks or missed opportunities are most prevalent and severe at our organization today?
- What relevant behaviors could training seek to change?
  - Which specific behaviors, by which specific roles, have the greatest correlation to the likelihood and severity of our most pressing risks?
  - Which forms of misconduct or neglect could be most disastrous to our customers, our employees, or our bottom line?
  - If we could help employees solve just one real problem they encounter in this area, what solution would have the biggest impact?
  - Of these behaviors, which are we most able to affect through training?
- How would we know if the training achieves the desired behavior change?
  - What metrics exist or could be created that show whether training moves the needle toward the desired behavior changes?
  - With these key metrics in mind, what can we do to ensure the maximum impact when comparing pre- and post-training measurements?
  - Which specific behaviors, by which specific roles, have the greatest correlation to the likelihood and severity of our most pressing risks?

These considerations may feel like common sense, and their appeal should be immediately obvious to any instructional designer or compliance expert. If we can align our training to real business risks, we can ensure it is relevant. If we can build that training around behavior-based objectives, we can ensure it is applicable. And if we know how our success in transferring those objectives will be measured, we can ensure the training is effective in meeting its ambitions or notice when there is a need to improve it and try again.

The appeal of the analysis form lies in its apparent simplicity, but when they first attempt to use the form on a real compliance training project, many practitioners will soon remember that human behavior is anything but simple. After initial enthusiasm over the immense promise of a behavior-based approached, many instructional designers and SMEs encounter a second stage of despondent head-scratching. "If I knew what behaviors need to change," many say, as they stare at the blank boxes on the second page of the form, "I'd already be changing them!"

Luckily, like any other language or skill, use of the Compliance Training Analysis Form can be learned, and it can become a powerful tool to anyone who is willing to persist beyond their first introduction. With a little practice and a dogged dedication to filling it out in earnest for every new compliance project, the blank spaces on the form become much less daunting. After enough successful projects, you may even find that the form itself is no longer necessary. Eventually, you will have internalized enough behavioral trends to quickly assess any new subject and identify likely learning opportunities in an instant.

If you're not already at the stage of immediate recognition, or if you need to get the buy-in of key stakeholders by allowing them to draw their own behavioral conclusions, there are two approaches you may find useful in overcoming any initial blocks and getting the behavioral juices flowing. For our purposes, we describe the two approaches as top down and bottom up. Depending on your organization, your stakeholders, and the constraints of the specific subject, you may find that both approaches could launch your next compliance training project on a strong behavioral footing.

Top-Down Behavioral Analysis

The top-down approach derives behavioral learning opportunities from the perspective and priorities of your organization's senior leaders. It allows your most strategic stakeholders to have a voice in the compliance training project, and it guarantees that your final deliverable is aligned with your organization's mission. Further, because the approach is so heavily informed by your executives and their needs, you increase the odds of broader executive buy-in for the program, which is critical to ensuring lasting change. These individuals can be powerful champions or detractors for any training program, and consulting them early is the best way to keep them on your side.

There are countless ways to execute a top-down approach, but if you have the option of convening an in-person meeting of key executives and stakeholders, you may be surprised at how much of the analysis and design phases of your project can be completed in just two focused hours. This is especially true if you structure the time carefully, as shown in the four-step process outlined below.

Step 1: Identify Risks

After a brief introduction to the category by the appropriate subject matter expert, including any pertinent content requirements you captured on page 1 of the analysis form, ask the senior leaders what they perceive to be your organization's most pressing risks in this category.

Before diving into a group discussion or trying to fill out the form together, it's often useful to include some time for individual reflection. A simple post-it note exercise can help generate a wide range of ideas and prioritize the most pressing needs:

1. Give each participant a stack of sticky notes and a pen.

2. Ask each participant to work alone and write at least five potential risks on five sticky notes. Alternatively, you can give them a set amount of time and ask them to list as many risks as they can think of.

3. As they finish, ask each participant to place their sticky notes on a designated wall.

4. As a debrief, organize the sticky notes into recurring categories of risk. Use the consolidation process to clarify any vague risks and tease out specific fears or observations that lay behind generic descriptions. A mutual understanding of

exactly what each risk means, and what it looks like in the daily reality of your business, will be critical when you move into the next step.

5. Now that you have a clear visual depiction of your perceived risks and a shared understanding of what each risk means, have a large group discussion to prioritize the three most pressing risks.

6. List these risks on the Compliance Training Analysis Form, then use the scale to rank the prevalence and severity of each. If two stakeholders disagree about how to rank a specific risk, give the group time to discuss and reach a consensus.

7. Have the room select the most severe and prevalent risk from the list. Which would be most damaging and most likely to occur in the current climate? Reducing this risk will then become the desired outcome for the rest of the compliance training project.

Step 2: Diagram the Causes That Contribute to the Risk

Now that you have a clear idea of the training project's desired outcome, you and your panel of leaders can work backward to identify behavioral learning objectives to help reduce the likelihood or severity of that risk.

This stage can be a daunting prospect at first, as many risks can feel mysterious and beyond our tangible control. To move from vague risks to actionable opportunities, break your chosen risk down into its component causes. Unlike broad risks, these causes should be specific, measurable, and easy to affect.

A fishbone diagram is the perfect tool for this exercise, and it can be highly effective when facilitated thoughtfully. For example, you can't teach someone to be a good basketball player. But if you break the definition of *good basketball player* down to its components, you will soon find an ample list of behavioral learning objectives that could help you achieve your desired outcome. For example, you could make someone better at shooting left-handed layups by giving them a technique lesson and asking them to shoot 100 layups every day for a month. That skill (left-handed layups) is specific, relevant to your goal, and highly learnable, which makes it the perfect candidate for a strategic learning solution.

For an example in the world of compliance, let's explore cyber security. After completing the initial risk analysis exercise as the kick-off meeting for this year's mandatory cyber security training project, your senior leaders all agree that a public data breach is the most serious and prevalent risk for your organization in this area. The desired outcome of your training program is to reduce the risk of such a breach, and you will need to focus on the behaviors that could cause or prevent such a breach if you want that outcome to be successful.

Broadly speaking, as seen in the fishbone diagram in Exhibit 5-1, there are two potential causes of a data breach. Your systems may be hacked directly by exploiting technical vulnerabilities, or they may be hacked socially by exploiting your employee's vulnerabilities. These still aren't specific or actionable enough to count as good behavioral objectives, but we're getting closer!

Exhibit 5-1. Cyber Security Fishbone Diagram

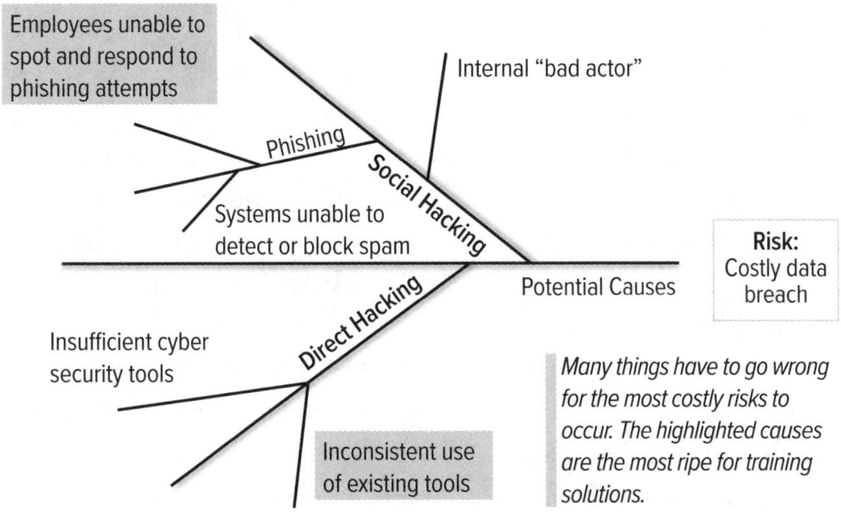

Employees unable to spot and respond to phishing attempts

Internal "bad actor"

Phishing

Social Hacking

Systems unable to detect or block spam

Potential Causes

Risk: Costly data breach

Insufficient cyber security tools

Direct Hacking

Inconsistent use of existing tools

Many things have to go wrong for the most costly risks to occur. The highlighted causes are the most ripe for training solutions.

As you continue to map further causes and sub-causes, your diagram will gradually become more complex. These smaller bones in the growing skeletal fish are where behavioral needs usually start to become clear, somewhere around the second or third order of the causal chain. For example, what are the causes that could lead to direct hacking? For one, you may not have sufficient resources and tools to stay ahead of cybercriminal technology. If your group of stakeholders believes this might be the case, it certainly warrants further investigation.

Perhaps a special training course is needed for IT executives or your board of directors to convince them of the need for further investment, or perhaps all training should be postponed until the tools and systems are in place that could allow that training to be successful. This is the beauty of having all your senior leaders in the same room. The training team cannot typically make such a determination on its own, but the senior leaders on your compliance committee could, especially if they believe they have uncovered the need themselves.

But insufficient resources are only one potential cause of direct hacking. Another may be that your company's IT professionals aren't consistently applying the safeguards available to them. If you think this is the case, focused systems training for your IT professionals could be an excellent way to reduce your risk.

One thing you'll notice about these examples and the Compliance Training Analysis Form itself is that behavior is meaningless without context. For the concept of behavior-based learning to be useful, we must think of behavior as a specific thing that a specific person chooses to do or not do in a specific situation. Because human action is most often taken in direct response to our situations, it is meaningless to think of behavior as something that can exist independent of or above the roles, responsibilities, and daily realities of individual employees.

This is why the Compliance Training Analysis Form prompts you to think not only of opportunities for behavior change, but also the specific roles for which those opportunities will be pursued. A multi-pronged program, with diverging objectives prioritizing the right content for the right people, is likely the only way that training can have a meaningful impact in the real world.

Step 3: Prioritize Your Most Relevant and Learnable Objectives

Some paths through your fishbone diagram will provide better opportunities for behavioral learning solutions than others. For example, the number one cause of social hacking is phishing attacks, during which innocent users from anywhere in your organization can be convinced to click links or divulge passwords that compromise your system's safeguards. Phishing is an especially annoying problem for cyber security teams to face after investing in state-of-the-art firewalls and technological safeguards. It's akin to bolting your front door with 10 locks, but leaving a back window wide open.

Luckily, phishing can easily be prevented through training. If you can help your entire population spot the signs of phishing and react appropriately if they think phishing has occurred, you can dramatically reduce the overall risk of a data breach. That's the kind of objective that a good online video or tutorial is perfectly able to address, and the success or failure of that objective can be easily measured. Using the Compliance Training Analysis Form's terminology, those qualities make anti-phishing behaviors highly "learnable."

This bone in the diagram may hold your compliance training answer: Instead of another tutorial full of policy references and legal terms, why not focus this year's mandatory cyber security training exclusively on phishing? It's easy enough to ensure such a course would still meet the letter of the law as defined on page 1 of the form, and it will do more to meet the spirit of the law than any rote legal tutorial ever could.

If a given behavior is both relevant and learnable, it's a perfect candidate for inclusion in your final program.

Step 4: Define Your Metrics

Our behavioral approach to compliance training becomes especially attractive if we can prove that it works to change behavior. To ensure that proof is possible, it is wise to consider measurement options for your top learning objectives before your senior leaders leave the initial analysis meeting.

It may seem counterintuitive to begin discussing measurement before development has even begun, but there are two big reasons to address measurement ahead of design and development. First, as a practical matter, you need to know early what metrics already exist, what data must be captured now to show your pre-training state, and what new reports or tools might be needed to allow any meaningful measurement to occur. Second, and perhaps even more important, the existence or lack of potential measurement tools can be a useful tiebreaker when deciding which learning objectives your program will serve. Those objectives that you are most excited about measuring will naturally rise to the top of your discussion, allowing all stakeholders to leave the initial meeting with a clearer idea of what your compliance training program really aims to accomplish.

This focus on measurement isn't as cynical as it might sound. If our primary goal is to help people solve real problems, then we need to be sure our learning objectives are relevant and actionable. By more than mere coincidence, the most relevant and actionable learning objectives also tend to be the most observable, and therefore the most measurable.

By contrast, a self-evidently noble learning objective may be flagged as important by every stakeholder in the room, but if no one can articulate how they would know for sure if that objective was achieved, it's appropriate to ask why they believe it should be included in a learning program that's stated purpose is to change behavior. How can we change something if we can't even see it?

If it's not broken, as the old adage says, why fix it? Similarly, if the impact of a specific behavior isn't observable, what makes us think it's a problem worth fixing?

To help facilitate this important discussion, page 2 of the Compliance Training Analysis Form also includes space to list your metrics for success on each objective. This will help you prioritize your most actionable objectives now and eventually allow you to determine whether those objectives were met.

The Virtuous Cycle of Measurement

By setting out to measure the effectiveness of your training, you can prove the worth and outcomes of your current offerings. Open-ended post-learning assessments can also highlight improvement needs for future offerings, accelerating your analysis process and shifting your library more toward the real needs of your learners. If you're looking to unearth new, relevant problems to solve, measuring your existing solutions is a great place to start.

We'll cover post-training measurements in a later chapter, but discussing tentative metrics in the analysis phase, at the very beginning of the project, is more than just a head start. It's a necessary foundation for everything that follows.

Bottom-Up Approach to Mining for Behavior

While there is immense value in winning the buy-in of your senior executives first, the top-down approach may not be tenable for every project. You may not be able to gather the stakeholders you need at the same table, or your executives might be too disconnected from the daily work at your organization to effectively trace business outcomes back to employees' behavior on the ground. Instead, or in addition, you may find it useful to start some projects from the other end of the spectrum. After all, your employees probably know what they need better than anyone else ever could.

Whether you start with job shadowing, focus groups, or surveys, a willingness to step out and see the world from your learners' perspective usually pays dividends. If you ask learners what they would like to know, or what current pain-points they would like to avoid in a given compliance area, you may be surprised at how fruitful their responses can be.

This approach can be executed even more easily than the top-down approach we just discussed, requiring only three simple steps:

1. Convene a representative sample of your audience.
2. Introduce the subject of your training in five minutes or less. Ask what questions they have and ask what problems in that area they would like to see solved.
3. Listen.

The conversation isn't always productive, but sometimes a single response is insightful enough to drive the structure, content, and measurable outcomes of an entire course or program. Often, incorporating the learners' perspective will yield a learning experience far more engaging and impactful than anything an instructional designer or SME could have ever dreamed up in a vacuum.

For example, consider mandatory FERPA training at an average institute of higher education. The FERPA act requires specific protections for student data, including mandated compliance training for anyone who has access to such data. Many schools may meet this training requirement with a compliance tutorial that's full of acronyms, definitions, and consequences for unlawful disclosures. Such training may meet the organization's legal requirements, but it likely does nothing to change behavior, reduce risk, or solve problems. For that, you would first need to know what your real problems are.

If the instructional designer could get away from the SME's PowerPoint and talk to a few representative members of their audience, the problems would likely be readily apparent. They'd likely hear comments from employees in the registrar similar to these:

- *I hate FERPA. I can't do my job like I used to.*
- *People don't understand it.*
- *I've heard some of my employees tell students they can't confirm their grades over the phone because of FERPA; but I don't think that's part of FERPA at all.*
- *They keep changing what we're allowed to say and what we aren't, so I figure I better be safe and say nothing.*

And so, in five minutes on the floor with one department, you've found a relevant behavioral need desperately in need of addressing. These "FERPA false positives" are impeding customer service and daily operations and causing undue anxiety for your employees. Instead of another tutorial rife with legalese, why not focus this year's compliance opportunity on a course that helps student-support professionals meet common student requests within FERPA constraints? You don't even have to call it a

FERPA course—call it Student Support 101. You can focus the structure and content on resolving the questions you know your audience actually wants answered, and just be sure that the steps you recommend are fully compliant with all FERPA regulations.

A reluctant SME might argue that this has nothing to do with FERPA compliance or worry that it doesn't meet their full legal requirements, but the Compliance Training Analysis Form helps to appease those concerns. You know exactly what the law requires, thanks to page 1 of the form, so you can assure all your stakeholders that the delivered solution will still meet those core requirements, even if the tutorial is packaged and designed differently than in previous years.

And on page 2, you can work backward from the behavioral need you discovered to identify its relevant outcomes. Improved customer service is an obvious outcome that should excite most of your stakeholders, but it probably won't help much to engage your compliance SME, who is more concerned with managing risk. Luckily, a course built around customer service, rather than legal terms and definitions, would likely do more to reduce the chance of a FERPA violation, too.

This may seem counterintuitive at first, but history is rife with examples of overly strict rule interpretations producing unintended consequences. One of the most famous examples was provided by the British government during their colonial rule in India. In an effort to reduce the cobra population, they sensibly implemented a policy of paying individuals for dead snakes returned to the embassy, believing that the incentive would create a team of motivated snake hunters on the streets of Delhi. Instead, the rigid policy and misaligned incentives motivated citizens to create cobra farms, where they could breed more cobras to kill and sell for the bounty. When the government discovered this unintended consequence, they immediately ended the reward program. Lacking any further incentive, the farmers simply released their cobras back into the streets, leaving Delhi with an even more dangerous snake problem than it had when the policy started.

These kinds of counterproductive policies and incentives are at work in the corporate world every day. Organizations that rely too heavily on dogmatic adherence to policies and systems can spark the wrong kind of motivation in their audiences, leading to poorer performance and higher rates of misconduct. If people perceive a set of rules as cynical or overly burdensome, some will adhere to the rules anyway, at the expense of their own initiative and agency. Others will refuse to compromise their common sense and their own internal sense of right and wrong. These employees—ironically, the same employees who could be your most productive workers and most ethical leaders—learn only to game or ignore such a system.

If you interpret your FERPA training mandate with an emphasis on the most stringent rules and controls, for example, that training will be impeding your people from adapting to the needs of the moment and serving their customers, which is their core responsibility. Over time, people will come to see such training and your broader FERPA compliance program as invalid and impossible to appease, and they will learn to circumvent it or ignore it. In such a cynical, disconnected culture, FERPA violations would become even more likely to occur.

You can help your organization avoid this fate by ensuring that your training is enabling and supportive, not just restrictive. If you get the balance right, you will not only create training that is more welcomed by your learners and more advantageous to the broader mission of your organization, you will also do more to reduce the legal risk of a FERPA violation than a "thou-shalt-not" tutorial ever would.

Eliminating false positives and overly restrictive policy interpretations is a perfect example of the real value that compliance training can offer, but has rarely delivered in the past. And we would have never known that opportunity existed in our FERPA scenario if we hadn't left our office, moved beyond the focused perspective of our executives and SMEs, and listened to the voice of our learners.

Think Return on Investment

Another way to save compliance training is to start thinking about your total investment in your programs, and the costs those investments will help your organization avoid. This includes standard compliance costs—like settlements, fines, and auditing penalties—but also behavioral costs like inefficiency, ineffectiveness, turnover, or loss of customers and reputation. If you want to make your compliance training as valuable as possible, you'll want to emphasize the measurable objectives and outcomes that add the most real dollars to your ROI equation.

Return on Investment = Current Cost − (Investment + New Cost)

From Problems to Solutions

Whether you choose a top-down or bottom-up approach, you should leave the early days of your next compliance training project with a clear idea of the real needs an ideal program would address. Over time, you will find that the analysis process gets easier and easier. In addition to the SME and audience interviews we've already discussed, the data sources outlined in Exhibit 5-2 can be useful for generating theories of potential needs and validating those theories to ensure you direct your learners' attention to the most relevant and impactful targets.

Exhibit 5-2. Information-Gathering Sources

Good for Generating Theories	Good for Validating Theories
SME interviews	Help desk records
Senior leadership interviews	Incident logs
Job shadowing	Key performance indicators
Audience focus groups	Audience surveys
Organization or industry reports	Test cases

As your compliance training initiatives become more relevant, they will also become more popular. With that popularity, your efforts will begin to yield additional suggestions and requests from your audience. And so, as your pool of relevant content steadily expands, areas for further improvement will become more apparent. Once you start designing for behavior change, behavioral needs become easier and easier to find.

The Compliance Training Analysis Form in appendix 1 is an ideal way to launch that cycle. Completing the form, or completing a similar process that allows you to answer the same basic questions, is likely the most important step of any compliance training project. But it's also only the beginning.

The behavioral learning objectives we uncover are of little use if we can't actually hit them. Seeing the need for change is an important half of the battle, but to make those changes stick, we need to start thinking less like trainers and more like behavioral engineers or choice architects.

For that, we need to shift our attention to the true origins of human behavior, and the strategic learning solutions that can reliably influence those behaviors in the moment of need. Now that we know our initial and desired state, we'll spend the next four chapters discussing how to chart a path between the two.

Chapter 6

Belief, Culture, and the Levers of Human Behavior

"There's a small, well-known restaurant on San Pedro Avenue, one of the main thoroughfares through San Antonio, that serves great local cuisine at good prices," began Earnie Broughton, senior adviser with the Ethics and Compliance Initiative. He was recounting an anecdote of one of his favorite hometown restaurants, which bore surprising relevance to our discussion of learning and compliance.

"I was picking up my dinner one night," he explained, "when I noticed the place looked a little quieter than usual. The owner said things were going well at their other location, which was a little outside town, but orders had been down for months at this ideal spot, right on the most well-traveled road in the city. That made no sense to me at all."

When Broughton asked the owner how such a perfect spot could be struggling for business, he was surprised by the ease with which the man found the answer: "The city put a new median in the road."

The new median made it impossible to turn left directly into the parking lot, which customers had been able to do in the past.

"I just went down to the next light," Broughton explained. "You could easily take the back road into the lot, which added almost no time to the trip. But drivers don't make a full calculation in the moment. They just encounter an obstacle that changes their situation, even only slightly, and they decide to go somewhere else for dinner. Maybe without even noticing their decision."

Business had plummeted overnight according to the owner, just because of a little extra strip of concrete.

When he went back a few months later, Broughton was greeted by a line at the counter. The owner and his neighbors had petitioned the city to remove the median from the road, and the city agreed. "They took the median out on a Tuesday," Broughton said, "and business was back to normal by Wednesday."

Broughton paused, letting me draw my own connections between this tale of takeout traffic in San Antonio and the world of corporate compliance training.

"I think about that median all the time," he concluded. "It's a perfect example of how small changes can have a big impact on human behavior. Those are the kind of changes we need to build with our compliance programs."

In the previous chapter, we unearthed important behavioral needs in our organizations. Addressing those needs is not a matter of building another tutorial, adding another policy slide, or forcing more heavy-handed training on our employees. Instead, we must observe the traffic patterns that govern their daily lives, and add or remove small barriers and nudges that can help them arrive more consistently at the right destination. These initiatives don't need to be big, expensive, or difficult to build—they just need to be placed strategically, with a keen understanding of human behavior and its primary causes.

The Complex, but Mostly Predictable, Origins of Behavior

In the novel *The Idiot,* Fyodor Dostevesky (1868) reminds us that "the causes of human actions are usually immeasurably more complex and varied than our subsequent explanations of them."

Research in behavioral economics, choice architecture, and persuasive design has boomed in recent decades, generating daily epiphonies that further illuminate the once dark and mysterious origins of behavior. However, any attempt to simplify human nature is likely prone to oversimplification. Whatever the latest self-help headlines or pseudoscience text books may tell you, human beings remain, above all else, complicated.

If we embrace the inherit complexity of behavior, we can still draw useful conclusions. We don't need to understand every aspect of every choice to help influence those choices, and we don't need to reduce our notion of humanity to a species of mindless, reactionary automatons to make some reliable predictions about how most humans will respond to most situations or how learning might be able to influence those responses.

For our purposes, we will discuss human behavior as a complex interaction between five primary influences—culture, belief, context, habit, and motivation (Exhibit 6-1). We can hope to affect three of these influences directly through training. In some situations, all five influences will have a voice in guiding the final decision of the actor. In other situations, the cry of any single influence could be strong enough to drown out the others.

Exhibit 6-1. The Five Influences on Behavior

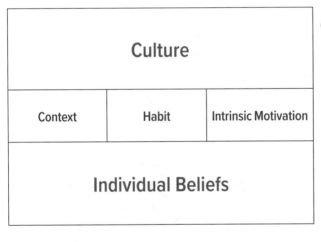

Culture		*Culture is shaped by collected behavior over time, and strongly influences behavior once set.*
Context	Habit	Intrinsic Motivation
		This is where we can create change.
Individual Beliefs		*Beliefs and values remain largely fixed with the individual, but may be acted on differently based on the other behavioral drivers at play.*

To briefly introduce these five influences, let's return to that median in San Antonio and explore how it would have elicited different reactions when different behavioral influences were at play.

- **Context.** The restaurant owner's depiction of the median and its consequences illustrates the critical role of context in our daily decisions. Adding a median in the wrong place changed the context in which individuals would choose their stop for dinner, and that slight context change was enough to produce a costly behavior change for a large portion of the customer base. However, this change in context would not have affected every customer equally. Context rules if all other things are equal, but things aren't always equal. The other four behavior influences may overrule context in some situations, and generate far different results.

- **Habit.** Habit, once set, can be stronger than context in governing our daily actions. For example, imagine someone who had been eating at the same Mexican restaurant every Monday night for 20 years. Do you think a median in the road would have diverted such a loyal customer? Brands spend fortunes cultivating customer loyalty because they know the answer to that question: A habitual customer is a reliable customer, even when other influences change.

- **Motivation.** True, intrinsic motivation is rarely called on in daily life. Reactionary, instinctive, habitual behavior is typically enough to get us through the day, without the time and effort required for willpower and rational decision making. But when we find ourselves truly motivated, we are capable of breaking entrenched habits and transcending our context, in limited sprints at least. And it doesn't always take that much to motivate us. For example, imagine that a friend told you last week about how great the burritos were at this Mexican restaurant. What if this friend further described the restaurant as a well-kept secret most people can't find. That simple challenge would likely be enough for you to find the restaurant on the map, make a plan to visit, and follow through on that plan, easily overpowering any minor contextual obstacles added to the road along your way.

- **Individual belief.** Beliefs are hard to change, as we will discuss shortly, but they are very powerful once set. For example, if you were a person who believed that this Mexican restaurant was by far the best in town, or who believed that sudden u-turns were perfectly acceptable and never ticketed, you would be less likely to be diverted by a minor change in context than someone who didn't share those beliefs.

■ **Culture.** Imagine that San Antonio was a less car-dependent city, instead benefiting from a culture where most people walk to work. In such a culture, a new median in the road would have little, if any, impact on behavior. Like individual beliefs, culture can be a dominant force in human decision making. It can affect context and the other three behavioral influences we've discussed, and it has understandably become a buzz-word for many compliance officers and organizations. But like beliefs, culture is difficult to change directly. Our goal should absolutely be to shape culture, but we need to take the long view. Culture is nothing more than a collection of be-haviors solidified over time. Small, strategic changes to those individual behaviors will eventually yield culture change too, at which point our ethics and compliance goals will become much easier.

Culture and beliefs are the foundation for everything else, but when it comes to individual behaviors in any given day, the mediating factors in the middle are our best opportunity to take the behavioral wheel. By focusing all your learning on influencing some combination of context, habit, and motivation, you can help ensure that wheel remains pointed in the right direction.

But before we move on to a detailed exploration of these three key behavioral levers, let's discuss the unavoidable constraints of culture and belief, and how they must inform our approach.

The Constraints of Culture and Belief

Ask any coach who has taken on the challenge of fixing a losing team, any CEO who's been hired to right the ship at a floundering organization, or any teacher who has tried to convince a disinterested student to care more about academic success; culture and belief are vital to the success of any endeavor, and they are difficult if not impossible to change.

Myriad biases and blind spots cause humans to favor the status quo, as individuals and as groups, even when there is clear potential for improvement. No psychological rule defines this inertia more succinctly than the confirmation bias, which serves as the foundation for implicit racial and gender bias, superstition, self-fulfilling prophecies, the over-inflated power of first impressions, and many other errors of human judgment.

Put simply, confirmation bias explains that beliefs often influence how evidence is perceived and interpreted, but that evidence rarely has any direct influence on beliefs. If highly partisan individuals are presented with a convincing piece of evidence against their presidential candidate, for example, they are much more likely to ignore or explain away the evidence than to switch party affiliations. This favoring of existing theories over new evidence is true for democrats and republicans alike, and with an understanding of the physiological processes of the brain, it's easy to see why.

MRI scans of the brain during the above scenario reveal a maelstrom of neural activity in the moment the conflicting evidence is introduced. Our brains don't like to hold two mutually exclusive ideas at once, and when you force it to try by presenting contradictory evidence to a long held belief, it becomes highly agitated. The ensuing neural battle is called cognitive dissonance, and the desire to reduce this dissonance is thought to be one of humanity's most fundamental psychological drivers.

This reduction in dissonance is exactly what scientists observed when participants in the above study explained away the evidence against their candidate, typically by justifying the evidence with broader context, excusing it as a simple mistake, or denying it as fake news. The neural storm within these participant's brains immediately subsided, returning to the comfort of their familiar status quo. It's worth noting that this need to reduce dissonance typically only works in one direction. Belief triumphs over evidence nearly every time.

This unconscious rule of human decision making wreaks a great deal of havoc in our world, including the perpetuation of harmful corporate policies, practices, and perspectives. But it survives as a mental process because it also offers real value.

For most of human evolution, fixing beliefs firmly in place has been a recipe for survival. If you saw a magician appear to levitate in a show, for example, it would be unwise to take that evidence at face value and change your long-held belief in gravity. If you did not have the confirmation bias protecting you, your plan to beat traffic by flying home would not end well. Much safer, in this case and many others, is to keep your existing beliefs and question the validity of the new evidence instead.

Transformative learning that changes long-held beliefs can happen, but it typically requires either an especially salient individual experience, or an especially pervasive change in a society's collective behaviors and perspectives. For example, citizens in West Africa changed their beliefs and burial practices after they were convinced that their traditional method of handling the dead was accelerating the spread of Ebola. There was always strong evidence for changing the practice, but changing individual beliefs and the collective culture was a long, uphill battle. It certainly took more than a single pamphlet or an online video; it took painful firsthand experience and a broad, collective shift in cultural expectations. Such paradigm shifts are the only way new beliefs can ever arise, and they are critical to individual development and societal progress. They are also, by nature, exceedingly uncommon. Usually, paradigms don't shift. They don't even budge.

The moral for compliance training is simple: Don't expect a single course or tutorial to change long-held beliefs within your organization or shift a culture that has been learned through years of experience. Instead, as detailed in the following chapters, we must focus on changing the specific, individual behaviors that training has a real chance to influence. Beliefs and culture are mostly outside our control, but behavior can still be changed with small but powerful tweaks in your employees' context, habits, and motivations.

Before we move on to focus on these behavioral levers, we must remember that beliefs and culture have the constant ability to bolster or undermine everything we are trying to build. If the gap is too large between what your program is asking your employees to do and what their own values or culture are telling them to do, your program will lose that battle. On the other hand, if you can align your programs with existing culture and beliefs, that shared ground can decrease skepticism, increase buy-in, and dramatically improve the odds of relevant and lasting behavior change.

How to Align Training With Beliefs and Culture

Culture and individual beliefs play a dominant role in decision making, and they are generally fixed. We may hope that our collective learning efforts can move the cultural needle over time, but culture and beliefs should primarily be thought of as constraints within which our programs must operate, instead of outcomes they can hope to achieve.

The following four tips can help you build your compliance programs on shared ground, and reap the benefits of aligning learning with learners.

Stick to the Needs You Uncovered in the Analysis Phase

Nobody wants help fixing a problem they don't believe they have. Luckily, your work in the analysis phase revealed real needs that should naturally resonate with your audience. If you can focus all your learning objectives on the sweet spot where required compliance content and your employee's real concerns overlap, your content will be perceived as credible evidence that reinforces their existing beliefs, instead of contrary evidence that their brain quickly rejects or explains away.

Offer a Menu of Options

In the final chapter of this book, we discuss how adaptive learning can change compliance by tailoring relevant content to the unique needs of each audience member. But if your current tools don't allow for adaptive learning, you can achieve many of the same benefits by offering a degree of self-selection. For example, imagine a tutorial where users choose from three possible case studies, instead of sitting through all three. You not only minimize the load on their attention span and increase the odds of each learner experiencing the most relevant content; you also gain willing buy-in. The act of choosing their own path can translate to added interest and increased motivation to learn.

At Georgia Tech, we've recently taken this concept a step farther. As part of a required, campus-wide ethics campaign, we promoted a class that offered to help learners provide direct, ethical feedback in challenging situations. The two-hour course was not required or incentivized in any way, yet 117 individuals chose to enroll. We believe strongly in the andragogical value of that course, and we think the value this self-selected audience will provide to the campus community will be stronger than a universally required, one-size-fits all, online version of the same content would have been.

Some core compliance content will always be required, but by making as much as possible optional, we allow our learners to decide what they need and what they don't, maximizing the behavioral return on their time and ours.

Avoid Framing Objectives in Terms That Divide or Threaten Your Audience

Some compliance subjects are loaded with sociopolitical implications, creating a minefield of sensitive beliefs that could easily derail your learning outcomes. Sexual harassment training is a perfect example. By frequently painting women as victims and men as cartoonish abusers, traditional harassment training has turned off many men who don't see themselves in either label, and who feel threatened by the insinuations.

"Since the training is threatening who you are, a defense mechanism is to say this is illegitimate," said University of Wisconsin professor Shannon Rawski in a 2017 interview with the *Washington Post* (McGregor 2017).

Rawski studied employees' reactions to harassment training for her doctoral dissertation, finding that it can be far more effective to focus harassment training on topics like bystander intervention, which appeal to people's deeper, more universal beliefs.

By focusing on core values the majority of your audience is likely to share—instead of loaded or contested beliefs that make some of your audience feel threatened, devalued, or alienated from your content—you have a far better chance of actually preventing harassment.

Let Your Learners Create the Frame

The good news about confirmation bias is that it doesn't only apply to existential, long-held beliefs. We form new beliefs about the world all the time, every time we encounter something or someone new. When these meetings occur, we form an initial theory quickly and then set about noticing evidence that supports that theory, ignoring everything else. You may have heard of this phenomenon in expert advice on everything from interviews to dating, all of which extol the awesome and potentially disastrous power of first impressions. And first impressions don't only count for people. The frame your compliance training establishes in its opening minutes is critical to how well the overall program is received.

If your opening frame fails to mesh with your learner's existing beliefs—perhaps telling an overly sensationalized story of sexual harassment, or an eye-catching statistic that sounds too shocking to believe—many of your learners will immediately form a theory that the content is misguided, misinformed, overly alarmist, or inapplicable to them.

Luckily, psychology provides an easy solution. Due to a combination of the confirmation bias and the availability bias, which we will discuss in the next chapter, humans routinely overestimate the likelihood of an event when asked to speculate. For example, every sports fan can think of at least one memorable example of a time when an underdog won a championship. These few memorable cases are enough to dramatically boost the odds given when individuals are asked to predict the likelihood of any given team winning a championship in the future, to a staggering degree. In fact, when researcher Craig Fox asked study participants to estimate the odds of eight different teams winning the NBA championship, one at a time, participants routinely gave each team higher chances of success than would be mathematically possible (Fox 1999).

By asking an open-ended question about an easy-to-imagine event, Fox prompted participants to adopt theories of circumstances under which each team could in fact win the championship, even the long shots. Once they formed those theories, participants' brains would set about gathering confirming evidence to support each theory. For example, if they were contemplating the odds of the worst ranked team winning it all, they might recall a single game they watched earlier that year where the team performed well, or recall other famous upsets from the past. All that mental effort led to a consistent overvaluing of the actual likelihood of each team winning, so much that the total odds assigned by the participants to all eight teams averaged 240 percent!

Instead of starting your next course with a compelling statistic about the scope of your problem, ask your audience to estimate the statistic from their experience. For example, ask your learners what percent of your employees are subject to sexual harassment over the course of their career. Chances are, at least one case will come to mind from the news or from personal experience, and the vividness of that example may lead your learners to overestimate the odds. Even your most skeptical learners are likely to offer a non-zero reply, allowing them to buy in to the fact that this is a real problem for at least some members of your organization, even if they don't believe it's as widespread as others might. "We believe that no one in this organization should ever suffer from harassment while doing their job," your course could confidently explain. "And the following learning experience will help you reduce the likelihood of harassment to zero."

Whatever preconceived notions your audience had about harassment, you just built a frame for the rest of the content that all your learners can buy into. That's the power of asking, instead of telling.

Pulling the Levers of Human Behavior

Imagine that individual beliefs are like a freight train barreling full steam ahead, entirely beyond our control. Culture is the track the train rumbles along, its rails laid long before we arrived, its iron outline inescapable. It's impossible to stop the train on your own or to change the track beneath it while it's running, but that doesn't mean you can't influence where the train ends up. If you can find a fork in the track, you may also find a lever. And the pull of the right lever can send even the most powerful train hurdling in a new direction.

Luckily, when it comes to employee behavior, there are three levers permanently within reach of a savvy instructional designer: context, habit, and motivation.

- Use your training program to shape the *context* around your learner in the moment of need, preventing many instances of misconduct before they are prompted by the environment.
- Alter your learners' *habits* by mapping their current cue-routine-reward cycles and making the adjustments needed to eliminate misconduct and replace it with more appropriate responses.
- Harness your learner's *motivation* and prompt self-directed change by appealing to the intrinsic human desire for purpose, autonomy, and problem solving.

But before we start pulling levers, we need to dwell a little longer on the distinction between outcomes and behaviors. We need to consider what kind of behavior changes we can realistically expect to achieve through these three simple mechanisms, and begin mapping our lofty outcomes back to the simple sub-behaviors we have the best chance of affecting.

Picking the Right Behaviors for Change

Winning any worthwhile change is usually a matter of targeting the right sub-behaviors. If you can identify behaviors that are directly correlated to your desired outcomes and ripe for change through context, habit, or motivated problem solving, you have found your path to success (Exhibit 6-2).

Exhibit 6-2. The Sweet Spot for Behavioral Learning

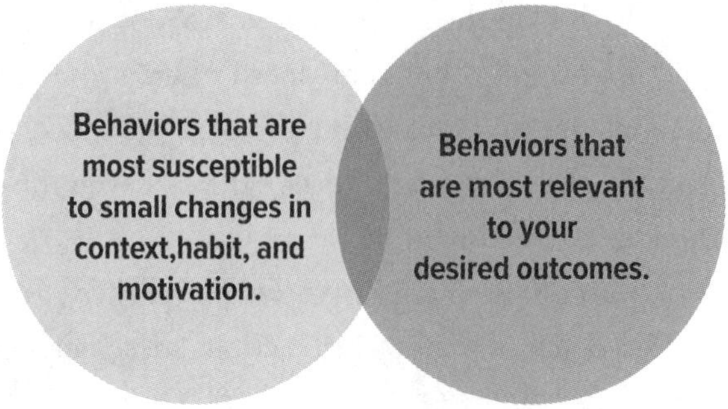

Behaviors that are most susceptible to small changes in context, habit, and motivation.

Behaviors that are most relevant to your desired outcomes.

Let's consider an especially irrational behavior that millions partake in every day: smoking. If you are a public health official whose desired outcome is to eradicate all smoking in your community, you have certainly set yourself a lofty goal! You may never reach 100 percent success, but if you can target the right sub-behaviors in the smoking life cycle with the right training initiatives, you can alter the broader behavioral landscape and make a measurable dent in overall rates.

For example, no one can become a smoker without trying their first cigarette. That specific behavior [*trying a first cigarette*]1, typically requires two sub-behaviors: [*someone has to offer a cigarette*]1a, and [*someone has to accept*]1b.

If you want to reduce the overall rate of smoking in your community, targeting either or both of these sub-behaviors would help:

[*someone has to offer a cigarette*]1a
Carton taxes may not be enough to stop addicted smokers from buying for themselves, but a sufficiently high tax may change the financial context enough to discourage sharing, making smokers less likely to offer nonsmokers a free cigarette.

[*someone has to accept*]1b
Adding graphic images to cigarette cartons showing smoking-induced illness, for example, may discourage some first-time smokers by changing the context in which the first cigarette is offered.

Neither of these contextual interventions is a magic bullet that can stop smoking completely, but you would expect their combined influence to at least modestly alter the real-world context in which the first cigarette is offered and accepted, which would certainly produce a non-zero effect on the overall likelihood of our targeted behavior, [trying a first cigarette]1. And if less people are trying first cigarettes, it won't be long before your overall smoking rates begin to drop.

If you want to take your success a step further, you could launch a parallel series of initiatives targeted at existing smokers, who are unlikely to be fazed by either of the above options. A picture on a carton isn't likely to exert much influence on a hardened smoker, as entrenched habits easily trump minor changes in context. To break habitual behavior, you must spark or support the smoker's own motivation to quit by appealing to their sense of purpose and self-improvement, and by structuring solutions that allow them to maintain a sense of autonomy over their lives and actions. You can also help by offering a replacement behavior that maintains their current cue-routine-reward cycle, such as substituting nicotine gum. Like the changes in context above, neither initiative will work for every smoker. But their existence makes it more likely that a few more people will choose to quit and be able to follow through, and even one fewer smoker is one step closer to your goal.

Like smoking, misconduct in any of our compliance categories typically occurs in a predictable life cycle of specific sub-behaviors, each a byproduct of specific behavioral influences in the moment of decision. And like smoking reduction, we have a better chance of winning change if we focus on adjusting those influences to alter those specific behaviors—one at a time, as needed by each audience—instead of trying to instill broader, generic training that overestimates human volition and misses the real root causes of so many of our actions.

When we apply our three behavioral levers at the right junctions—as shown in the GDPR case study in appendix 2—we can create holistic compliance training programs that do far more than check a box. We can guide decisions, shape behavior, and deliver the real value that compliance training was originally mandated to provide.

Chapter 7
Shaping Context: How to Make Good Conduct Instinctive

In his bestselling masterpiece on decision making, *Thinking, Fast and Slow,* Nobel Prize winner Daniel Kahneman explores a dual-system view of the human mind. System 1, the fast-thinking part of our brain, makes instinctual decisions based on habits, emotions, and contextual reactions. System 2, the slow-thinking brain, chimes in to provide rational justifications when our instinctual responses are called into question, or to perform more deliberate tasks and calculations when System 1 isn't able to act on autopilot.

For most of us, making a left turn when prompted by our car's GPS is an instinctive task, effortlessly performed by our System 1 brain. For others—like young children, those new to English, or my wife—interpreting and responding to the words "left" and "right" would require conscious effort from System 2.

Traditional compliance training often targets the slow-thinking part of the brain—System 2—with definitions, policies, statistics, and other overtly rational appeals. But in reality, most of the behavioral misconduct we are trying to correct is undertaken by the fast-thinking System 1 part of our brain, before System 2 ever has a chance to weigh in.

If most human behavior is akin to the rapid twitch movement of a humming bird, traditional compliance training is the slow-footed sloth that we have sent to chase it down. The results are predictably uninspiring.

If we really want to change behavior, we need to focus less effort on persuading the figurehead leadership of our System 2 brains, and more on guiding our System 1 autopilot—the real seat of power in our minds—to the right instinctive decisions. Instead of just preparing our learners to recite definitions or pass simple quizzes, we have to start influencing their gut reactions in the moment of need. In other words, we need to make our learning a lasting and persuasive aspect of their context.

The Hidden Power of Context

Imagine you volunteered for a scientific study of memory at a nearby university and arrive at the lab to find one other volunteer, a stranger to you, already in the waiting room. An experimenter soon arrives, introducing himself as the head researcher running the study, and splits you and the stranger into two separate roles. The stranger is taken to a small closet with a chair, where she is strapped to a series of live electrodes and asked to memorize a set of word pairs.

You are guided to the room next door, where you are given the same list of words and a switchboard marked with voltages. The experimenter explains that the purpose of the study is to measure the effects of electrocution on improving memory. He tells you that your role in the study is to test the stranger on the word pairs she's been memorizing, and to deliver a shock for every incorrect reply. For each new wrong answer, you are asked to increase the voltage by one increment, slowly climbing toward the top of the board, where the voltages are marked "potentially fatal."

The room is equipped with a speaker and a microphone, and you can hear the stranger beyond the wall howling in pain at each new shock, and she's soon pleading in a panic for the experiment to end. "Please continue," the researcher says, calmly. "The experiment requires that you continue."

What would you do in this scenario? Would you follow the researcher's instructions, continue the experiment, and deliver a potentially fatal shock to a total stranger? Or would your internal values and beliefs stop you from playing along in such a dangerous game?

If you are like most people presented with this thought experiment, you are probably appalled by the scenario and confident that you would never comply to such orders. And yet, when Stanley Milgram conducted this study in 1963, he found that only 37 percent of people actually lived up to that assumption in the moment of need. The rest—63 percent of participants—reacted obediently to their context, voluntarily continuing the experiment to its terrible end.

It's worth noting that these weren't "bad" people. Video from the study reveals a clear sense of moral struggle for all participants, despite their ultimate acquiescence. The participants expressed disbelief and deep remorse at their own actions during the experimental debrief, and did not seem to take the decision lightly. And yet, when compelled by the situation, many acted against their own best intentions.

Luckily, the stranger in the experiment was an actor and the shocks weren't real, but the lessons of the study were. As decision makers and compliance learning experts, we must resist the urge to blame misconduct on incomplete information, insufficient skills, or the malicious intentions of a few bad actors. Instead, we must think of misconduct as the byproduct of the specific situations that our learners find themselves in, and the context those situations create. If we can change the information that's most readily available to our learners in those situations, we can change the context. And if we can change context, we can change behavior.

Shaping Context, Shaping Behavior

For an example of how small changes in context can yield significant changes in behavior, let's return to the Milgram experiment we just discussed. As a simple thought experiment, ask yourself the following questions:

- Imagine the fatal shock levels were marked prominently on the switchboard, instead of the small, unassuming font used in study. Imagine there were large red signs on the door and above the board that read "DANGER: 95 percent of people who receive the highest level of shock immediately die as a result." Would you be as likely to flip the switch as you were in the original design of the experiment?

- Imagine there was no wall between you and the learner and you had to look her in the eye as you delivered each shock. Instead of hearing muffled cries through a speaker, you had to watch the anguish the switchboard was causing firsthand. Would you be equally as likely to continue the experiment?
- Imagine you had a partner with you at the switchboard, and that your partner stood up to the researcher and refused to continue. Imagine this partner—another volunteer, just like you—storms out of the room in disgust. Even if you stayed, would you be as likely to flip the final switch as you were in the original experiment?

If you think the above scenarios could make you even 10 percent more likely to resist flipping the final switch, then you intuitively know the behavioral value of context. Unfortunately, that value is frequently forgotten when we set about creating courses for our learners. Instead, we write objectives and craft exercises as if misconduct is due to a simple lack of knowledge or motivation, as if good and bad behavior originates entirely from within.

Too often, we ignore the competing priorities, conflicting messages, and daily realties that cloud our learners' judgment and prompt the wrong calculations in the moment of need. Context drives so much of our lives, and yet we find our training courses routinely whispering to the passengers in the backseat, as if the ability to recall definitions or decipher quiz questions gives them any hope of wresting away the wheel.

This error is not unique to the learning profession. In fact, the tendency to overvalue agency and undervalue context is so common that the psychological literature has dubbed it the fundamental attribution error. Instructional designers, SMEs, and every human on earth tend to ascribe too much weight to intentional System 2 decision making, and far too little to the instinctive System 1 influences that do so much of our deciding for us. The contextual factors that influence these gut decisions have enjoyed a recent spotlight in marketing, business, and healthcare, to sometimes astonishing results. There's no reason we can't use the same concepts to produce similar behavioral rewards from our compliance training. We only need to accept that our learners don't have an ethics problem, or even a decision-making problem.

They have an attention problem.

The Fundamental Attribution Error

Imagine you are cut off on the highway and have to slam your breaks to avoid crashing into the offender's rear bumper.

Rationally, while removed from the moment, you may recognize that traffic flow and other situational pressures can sometimes offer little choice but to change lanes quickly. You may even admit to having cut off a car at some point in your past, only, of course, because of the situation you were in at the time. And yet, when you find yourself suddenly cut off by a stranger on a busy highway, how likely are you to consider their situation?

Instead, might the colorful vocabulary you direct toward their back bumper reflect some potential value judgments, perhaps focusing on the driver's stupidity, carelessness, or selfishness? They cut you off, you seem to think, because they are the kind of person who cuts people off.

This routinely unbalanced attribution of behavior from situational to dispositional factors is what psychologists call the fundamental attribution error, and it doesn't only influence the way we view others.

It also causes us to fundamentally overvalue our own independence and undervalue the power of the situation on our own actions. For example, you may think today that you would have no problem sticking to a diet next week, because you know that you are committed to eating better and that you wouldn't willingly choose to engage in behaviors that undermine your own commitments. And yet, when confronted with tasty deserts at a dinner party next week, the situation may compel you to deviate from your diet far more readily than you'd like to hope.

If we want to help our learners avoid misconduct, we need to carefully consider how we contribute to their situation.

Biases, Heuristics, and the Three Most Powerful Forms of Context

Human beings are lazy decision makers, as Kahneman's central thesis suggests, but not in a bad way. We simply cannot afford to stop and perform a careful, conscious calculation for every single decision we're confronted with on a daily basis. The results would be paralysis, chronic indecision, and a serious dip in future dinner party invitations.

To cope with limited mental resources and seemingly unlimited demand, we take short cuts, adopt broad ground rules, and delegate as many judgments and decisions to our unconscious brain as possible. In Daniel Kahneman's words, we rely on System 1. We can't change the way our brains make these instinctive calculations—that would be swimming upstream against millennia of successful evolution—but we can change the information that's plugged in.

To function, our System 1 brains rely on few quick rules of thumb—known as heuristics—that instantly tell us what to pay attention to and what to ignore in any given situation. These simple heuristics usually lead our gut straight to the right decision, without any need for data tables or philosophy text books. We find ourselves doing the right thing instinctively, nine times out of 10, without breaking a cognitive sweat. But when our System 1 autopilots fail, they can fail spectacularly.

Our job as learning professionals is not to replace System 1, but to help it succeed 10 times out of 10. By focusing on the heuristics and biases that govern instinctive decision making, we can predict where our brains are most likely to misfire and which learning and development solutions are most likely to help. Thus, the remainder of this chapter will explore:

- the availability bias and how microlearning can help ensure your content remains a potent aspect of your learners' context
- the affect heuristic and how storytelling can increase retention and persuasion by appealing to your learners' strongest emotions
- the power of social influence, and how your depiction of your learners' peers can increase or decrease the likelihood of behavior change.

By understanding these basic ground rules, we can begin to see how behavior is really determined in the moment of need, and how we may be able to shape it.

Availability Bias, Microlearning, and the Loudest Voice in the Room

Imagine you were a perfectly rational decision maker who enjoyed the occasional glass of milk. At a modern grocery store, you have no less than

20 milk options available to you in the dairy aisle. If you wanted to make the most rational choice possible from these options, what information would you consider?

Taste is important, but obviously subjective. More objective information might include the milk's nutritional content, the commitment of its producers to sustainability and animal well-being, the bottler's adherence to food safety standards, the volume of milk in each container, and, of course, the price.

To make the best possible decision, you would need to assign a weight to each of these categories, establish a basic rubric for scoring within each category, and find all the data needed to calculate the aggregate scores and determine the best overall selection. That would be the fairest, most rational thing to do. So, when was the last time you brought your milk spreadsheet to the grocery store?

Instead, for most of us, the process of selecting milk involves little more than grabbing the same bottle we bought last time, possibly checking the expiration date before we throw it in the cart if our mental capacity in that moment allows such a luxury. This is behavior by habit, as we'll discuss in the next chapter, but where did that habit start? Did you at least use your faithful spreadsheet to make your first milk decision?

Again, probably not. Instead, you likely grabbed the milk that had the most attractive label, at the most readily available height on the shelf. Or you may have noticed and grabbed the most popular milk that covered the most space on the shelf. Or perhaps there was an especially enticing sale during that first trip to the grocery store, prompting you to grab the milk with the big, eye-catching sale tag, perhaps creating your habitual choice for years or decades to come. That is the power of context, and the value of highly available information.

Context is powerful because attention is finite. To avoid wasting any of that attention, human beings have learned to prioritize only the information that rises to the top. We don't make our decisions based on the most complete, accurate, or relevant information. Instead, the majority of our decisions are based only on the information that is most available.

Availability Bias

Our brain is selective in where it affords its attention. When making decisions, instinctively or rationally, we only tend to consider the most "available" evidence, rather than the most comprehensive or empirically sound evidence. Specifically, the readiness with which evidence for a decision comes to mind is determined by two availability factors: salience and prevalence.

Like most biases, the benefits and evolutionary origin of availability is easy enough to imagine. If you were an early human learning to navigate a dangerous, complex world, you would do best to pay attention to the causes that have the most serious effects, and also the cause-and-effect relationships that you encounter most often. For example, if a friend ate a strawberry and died shortly thereafter, the extreme salience of that information would likely keep you from eating strawberries in the future. Similarly, if you notice that you get a painful stomachache every time you try another breed of berry, the prevalence of that information will soon help you to stop eating them too. On the other hand, if you only occasionally get sick after eating a banana, and you never observe anyone else dying from it, you might never get around to considering whether you should also cut bananas from your diet. Instead, like your modern human equivalents, you would simply continue with the status quo until more salient or prevalent information convinced you to change.

If we want people to make ethical decisions, ethical values need to be mentioned and rewarded at least as often, and as saliently, as the core business drivers we harp on every day. Otherwise, when priorities conflict, the availability bias will drown out ethical considerations.

Think about it like this: Is a salesperson at your organization more likely to be chastised or fired for speaking to a co-worker with a lack of civility, or for losing a big client or failing to meet their next sales quota?

One thing is certain: The fast-thinking side of the brain already knows the answer to that question, and your employees' behavior will respond in kind.

As learning professionals, we don't control performance management, and we can't decide what behaviors are incentivized in our organizations. But we can ensure our learners hear the most important messages often. Perhaps even often enough for that information to be among the most available in their minds when the moment of decision making arrives. This is the immense promise of microlearning.

Microlearning

An industry-wide shift in learning and development away from time-consuming, away-from-work learning experiences and toward small, targeted solutions delivered often enough to become part of the learners' daily context. Instead of an intensive, week-long manager training program, a microlearning approach might encourage managers to participate in five minutes of online content every day for a year. These microlearning events would focus on specific needs and behaviors—through a short video or email—with targeted measurements and interactions to strategically reinforce outcomes.

A two-hour online tutorial, taken once a year, has little chance of providing highly available information to our learners when it's needed. Unless the moment of decision fortuitously falls in the same day or week as the training, it's a safe bet that our information will have plummeted down the availability scale by the time it's really needed. If you want evidence, just try to imagine (without smirking) any employee ever refusing to engage in misconduct with the explanation, "I can't, an online tutorial I took last year told me not to."

The available information deficit of annual compliance initiatives is only compounded by the fact that long, catch-all training is likely to be perceived by the employee as boring and irrelevant. It also makes the information seem less salient, because if it was genuinely important, they'd be hearing about it much more often than once a year.

These problems can be solved by thinking of your compliance training initiatives as conversations to be sustained over time, instead of requirements to be completed at once. Microlearning is one of the most promising methods, but it's not the only option, and it may not be possible at every organization. If you know the struggle of getting 10,000 people to complete a simple compliance program within an annual compliance window, you can imagine how impossible it could be to get those same 10,000 people to log in to your system and complete a new micro-course every day or week. Getting there requires the right tools and a wholesale shift in the way your organization thinks about learning; neither of those can be forced or fixed overnight.

But that doesn't mean you can or should give up on availability. Even if you don't have the resources or organizational buy-in to make a full-scale shift to microlearning, you can still find ways to incorporate some of microlearning's most impactful principles into your traditional learning systems and programs. For example, if your SME wants to include multiple case studies or scenarios for the same objective within an annual tutorial, you could best leverage your learners' attention by leaving only one case study in the main course, and developing another for use as a stand-alone follow up. This makes your SME happy by including everything they want, without further bloating a course that's probably already too long. As an added benefit, you could email the follow-up case study to your learners a few months after the annual compliance window ends, reinforcing the content and its perceived importance. If you have enough content, you could even send similar emails once a month, sustaining the conversation and dramatically increasing the availability of your compliance message in your learners' daily context.

You don't even need a fancy LMS to host and track the new micro-content. You already tracked completion of the annual tutorial for the lawyers' benefit. Now that the box is checked, you can focus your learning and development effort on delivering the message your learners really need to hear, in whatever way they are most likely to hear it. Post the content to YouTube, embed it in email, or leverage any communication tool you have at your disposal that can help sustain the conversation.

This technique, as part of a multi-pronged approach, can make your compliance information much more available in the moment of need, and make the voice of compliance one of the loudest, most frequently heard voices in your organization. The trick is to start thinking like an advertiser: If you want to capture the attention of your audience, get your message in front of them as often as possible.

Other Ways to Leverage the Availability Bias

Microlearning is just one way to keep your message in front of your learners. If you want your training content to play more of a role in your audience's decision making, you just have to move your content closer to those decisions.

Add Signs and Collateral

Take your message beyond the confines of your classroom or tutorial and make it a permanent part of your learners' physical context. Work with your communications team to review an inventory of potential channels in your organization—postcards, electronic message boards, event announcements, website banners—and use as many platforms as possible to expand the reach of your learning.

Embed Training in the Moment

The annual compliance window is a terrible way to spread a message. If possible, strive for rotating requirements that move your learning nearer the moment of need. For example, if you have training regarding acceptable gifts in the procurement process, it would be best to require that training as part of the workflow for initiating a new RFP, right when that content is most likely to be needed. This is a much better approach than subjecting your entire audience to the training during the same annual window and hoping they remember the content by the time its applicable to them.

Provide Train-the-Trainer Resources

Enlist managers and other leaders to help you continue your message beyond the formal training event. A simple collection of resources—like Q&As, follow-up videos, or structured group exercises—can equip your advocates with the tools they need to build on your learning and keep your information at the front of your learner's mind.

Create a Blog or YouTube Channel

The most effective learning plans blur the line between traditional training and communications. Instead of focusing all your attention on what can be tracked in your LMS, consider taking the most important parts of your message directly to your learner, wherever they already are. Adding a monthly video to a distributed YouTube channel, for example, can reinforce the importance of your message between your mandatory compliance windows. The lack of a "box to be checked" may also win more trust and interest from your learners, and demonstrate to lawyers, judges, and auditors how seriously your organization is taking the call for real behavior change.

Be Salient

Due to competing business priorities and the limited hours in a day, you may never be able to get your message in front of your learners as often as they need to see it. But prevalence of information is only one aspect of its availability. You can make the most of the time you have by making your individual messages as memorable and salient as possible, as we will discuss in the following section.

Affect Heuristic, Storytelling, and the Lasting Power of Emotion

If you, like me, enjoy an occasional hike in the woods, you may have found yourself checking for tick bites a little more often than usual in the summer of 2018. At least you would have if you were as susceptible to the affect heuristic as I am.

In response to a somewhat frightening CDC report on the rising rate of tick-borne illness, news outlets from CNN to the *New York Times* were running summer headlines like "Tick Infections Spreading Rapidly in U.S." and "Hikers Beware: Ticks More Deadly Than Ever Before."

Blaming warmer temperatures and increased jet travel, the authors of these articles juiced their stories with salient examples, like a woman in Mississippi who died from tick-induced Bourbon virus, and a realtor in Maryland who woke up covered in hives after being bitten by a lone star tick—leaving her with a bizarre, life-threatening allergy to dairy and red meat.

As someone who enjoys living, as well as the occasional hamburger, those stories got my attention. They were filled with ominous lines like "She thought she was going for a safe walk in the woods," and "She had no idea how long she would feel the effects of that tiny bite." Not to mention the disturbing, visceral images of magnified ticks near exposed human skin. As a result, I stopped several times during my walks that summer to inspect small sensations I felt on my arms and legs. Each time I looked down, I hoped I wouldn't see a tick burrowed into my skin, but thanks to the vividness of the stories and their effect on my imagination, I always expected I would.

In an effort to restore my fleeting sanity, I returned home from one such walk to confirm just how afraid I should be. The results of my search were immediately reassuring. While tick-related illnesses have indeed tripled over the last several years, they are still a relatively low risk. While Bourbon virus can be fatal, there are still less than 100 confirmed cases a year in the United States. Alpha-Gal syndrome, which can cause severe meat and dairy allergies, is so rare that the total case number is not even counted by the CDC. Even more encouraging, its debilitating symptoms are only occasionally permanent, and most often disappear within a few months!

For comparison, more than 5,000 people die from choking on food each year in the United States, making eating a much more prevalent threat to my survival. Yet, while I still can't go for a walk in the woods without stopping to check at least once for ticks, I never stop to consider the threat of choking before gnawing on a steak or devouring a peanut butter and jelly sandwich. This discrepancy is partly due to habit; I spend more time eating than I do walking in the woods, so my habits around eating are far more entrenched. Contextual cues are most powerful in areas where we don't already have entrenched habits, especially if those cues are designed to maximize our attention.

The news reports I was hearing that summer were so effective in changing my behavior—prompting a spray of bug repellent every time I left the house, without fail—because they were especially sensational. They told me a scary story, and they told it well.

Affect Heuristic

The availability of evidence is determined by its frequency and by its sensationalism. The affect heuristic explains that sensational stories—based on people like us, risks we might face, and strong emotional appeals—have far more influence on our decision-making process than objective statistics or dispassionate reason.

Stories can be powerful and lasting behavioral drivers, often setting the most available information in a person's mind for years or decades to come. The most highly affective stories can permanently alter the context of their audience—and the behaviors that context elicits—even if only experienced once.

Joanne Cantor, professor emeritus of communications sciences at the University of Wisconsin-Madison, confirmed this power with a fascinating follow-up study to Steven Spielberg's 1977 classic, *Jaws*. The film imagines the story of a great white shark terrorizing beach goers in a small New England town, and its tone and directorial style offer a master class in affect. When Cantor conducted her study 25 years after the film's release, she could still measure its impact: 43 percent of viewers reported an enduring fear of swimming, even though none of them had seen the film for at least seven years. That is the lasting power of a truly affecting story (O'Connor 2013).

We may not have the skills or budget of Steven Spielberg, but affective storytelling techniques are well within reach of any instructional design team. For example, consider the core story element of suspense.

A good story begins with a beginning that feels like a story: a call to action, a sudden conflict, a hint of ominous events to come. It has to hook the audience's attention and allow them to begin imagining an ending, while keeping at least some of that ending a mystery. Spielberg famously builds suspense in *Jaws* by showing the gruesome effects of the shark in the opening scene, but not allowing the audience to see the shark itself until near the end of the film.

Simple foreshadowing can achieve similar suspense in an e-learning tutorial, or even in a passage of written text. Starting an article about tick bites with the line, "She thought it was just a normal tick bite, but woke up that night covered in hives," naturally builds suspense by suggesting a serious ending, without telling us exactly what that ending will be. This engages the brain in speculation and problem solving, both of which make your learner more engaged in your content. That engagement makes your information more available in the moment of need, which makes your desired behavior change more likely to take hold.

Lisa Cron's *Wired for Story: The Writer's Guide to Using Brain Science to Hook Readers From the Very First Sentence* is a great resource for making your learning stories more suspenseful and engaging, and more likely to stick in your learners' minds.

Storytelling isn't a foreign language. We learn through stories as children, we keep our families and friends together with stories, we create our identities with stories. The trick to telling a good story is simply to try. And yet, so many compliance tutorials continue to be organized around lists instead of stories, full of rational appeals and dictionary definitions, totally absent of emotion, characters, suspense, or context. If you want to make compliance training that resonates with your audience, replacing your policy and definition slides with story slides is a great place to start.

Tips for an Affecting Compliance Story

Whether using video, animation, or simple still images—whether planning a feature length plot to unify an entire course, or a series of vignettes to underscore key objectives—the following tips can help make your stories as affecting as possible, giving your message a chance to become the most available information in your learners' minds for months or years to come.

Truth Is Stronger Than Fiction

The staying power of *Jaws* is partially due to the fact that sharks actually exist, and that shark attacks occasionally happen. Lon Chaney's classic *The Wolf Man* also features suspenseful storytelling, but I don't know many adults who refuse to walk outside at night in fear of wolf people.

Telling a story doesn't mean making up a fantasy. Many well-intended instructional designers have attempted to liven up their boring compliance offerings with elaborate parodies or humorous flights of fancy, like an impressive course I once saw on office dynamics where all the co-workers where Tolkien fantasy creatures. The novelty of such courses may elicit a little more attention from your learners—possibly even a chuckle—but without relevance and plausibility, they are no more likely to stick in your learners' minds.

True stories in the compliance space are easy to find, and often rife with enough suspense and tragedy to form a compelling, lasting narrative.

Fear Sells

There is a reason that political parties spend so much more of their money on negative attack ads than on positive candidate statements. If I want to drive you to get out and vote for me, the best motivator I have is to make you scared of what my opponent might cause you to lose.

The tendency of human beings to be roughly twice as motivated by potential losses than by potential gains is called the loss aversion principle. In addition to explaining why habits tend to stick forever, which we'll discuss in the next chapter, the principle explains why stories tend to capture so much of our attention. Every good story is driven by a conflict, and a conflict is nothing more than a potential loss.

To win and keep your audience's attention, dial up the stakes. If you can make them feel the real cost of noncompliance—to their safety, values, or livelihood—you can motivate change.

A Picture Is Worth a Thousand Words

A story doesn't have to have a beginning, middle, and an end. Suspense and conflict can sometimes be captured with a single line, a single statistic, or a single image.

Imagine a close-up of a depressed, anguished face with the title, "The Cost of Sexual Harassment," or a stark photo of a prosthetic limb with the caption, "I wish I'd paid more attention to forklift safety." Those images tell a story, and those simple visual stories may generate more attention from your learners than a full description or reenactment ever could.

Let Your Data Speak

A friend once dragged me to Home Depot to buy a crate of energy efficient light bulbs the day after watching the film *An Inconvenient Truth*. There were no characters or traditional plot in that film—it was essentially a recording of a live PowerPoint presentation—but Al Gore's expert use of suspense turned global warming into a compelling story; a story that filled my friend's shopping cart full of behavior change.

Don't think your next tutorial has to have an elaborate Hollywood script to capture the interest of your audience. Simple data can tell a very influential story if its presented with an understanding of conflict, suspense, foreshadowing, and a resolution that's still in doubt.

Choose the Right Characters

Don't let your audience off the hook by thinking, "This could never happen to me." For example, if the tick bite articles we discussed had focused on avid hunters or forest rangers, I might have paid less attention, thinking those people were fundamentally different from me—a casual, occasional hiker—and that their lifestyle choices made them more susceptible to the threat than I would be. Instead, the article was about a common realtor taking her dog for a walk one afternoon, a character I couldn't help but see myself in.

Make sure your characters resonate with your learners by making them realistic, sympathetic, and relatable. This is especially important given the immense pull of social influence on decision making.

The Pull of Social Influence

If you've ever raised a teenager, you're likely well-versed in the dangers of peer pressure. But social influence and conformity aren't relegated only to the domain of adolescence. Numerous studies in psychology and sociology have shown that the people around us remain one of the most dominant factors in human decision making throughout our lives.

Often referred to as the Asch Paradigm, the cognitive influence of groups was demonstrated perfectly in a series of experiments by Solomon Asch (1955). Presented with a fairly simple comparison task—as shown in Exhibit 7-1—99 percent of participants were able to reliably identify lines of matching length. Try it yourself now, which line on the right matches the length shown on the left?

Exhibit 7-1. Solomon Asch's Comparison Task

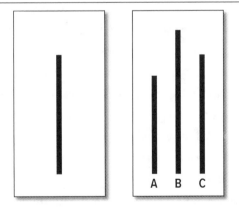

If you chose option C, congratulations! You're as perceptive as 99 percent of your peers!

However, even this straightforward, objective, and apparently easy judgment can be skewed dramatically by social influence. When participants were placed in a room full of actors espousing an incorrect answer—for example, a room with nine other people who were all strongly asserting that B was the matching line—only 25 percent of participants were able to reliably stand up to peer pressure and stick with their own superior judgment. The other 75 percent at least occasionally deferred to the apparent wisdom of the crowd over their own perception, and 5 percent trusted the opinion of the group over their own judgment every time.

Peer pressure, of course, isn't always negative. There are rational reasons for humans to pay careful attention to those around us. First, those around us may offer valuable information that we should include in our judgments. In the example above, participants may take the disagreement on the line test as evidence that their own senses are being deceived in some way, and that the other nine people know something they don't. Imagine you look out your apartment window one morning and notice that everyone on the street is carrying an umbrella. You may be wise to grab yours too, even if you didn't think the forecast called for rain.

Secondly, people can face serious social and economic consequences for standing in the way of consensus. While standing alone may sometimes yield benefits, the loss aversion principle causes our subconscious System 1 brains to fixate more on what we stand to lose by defying social norms, instead of what we stand to gain. This instinct is compounded by a known phenomenon called the Spotlight Effect, which causes most of us to believe that we are being observed far more closely by others than we actually are. So, even if we are 100 percent confident that it won't rain, we may choose to carry an umbrella anyway if we're worried we would otherwise be viewed as an outcast or an oddity and bared from social opportunities that might have presented themselves to someone more "normal."

These two factors—dubbed informational conformity and normative conformity—often come into play subconsciously, during fast-thinking System 1 decision making. In many experiments, participants have found their behavior influenced by the people around them without even noticing consciously that they were choosing the opinion of the herd over their own. Instead, it seems, the opinion of the herd unconsciously becomes the individual's opinion too. To put it in terms we're already familiar with, the behavior of those around us tends to become the most available information in our mind when it comes time to act.

As compliance training experts, we cannot live in denial of social influence. The behaviors our learners witness on their teams and in the broader organization will likely have a much stronger influence on their future decisions than any training course or tutorial ever could. If we truly hope to change behavior for the better, we need to start thinking of ways to influence our entire culture. If not, any positive changes we engender among individual learners will be trampled out by the perceived expectations of the group before they ever have a chance to take hold.

Tips for Wielding Social Influence

The following three tips can help you leverage social influence as a force for good instead of evil, sparking a virtuous cycle among your employee population that eventually reinforces itself.

Create a Social Frame

Perceived social norms are one of the most persuasive aspects of an individual's context, as shown in a useful experiment conducted by the Minnesota Department of Revenue.

In an effort to increase tax compliance, the department offered four kinds of messages to potential taxpayers. The first focused on the societal value of taxes and the greater purpose achieved by paying them, like paving roads. The second focused on the penalty for failing to pay taxes lawfully, and the third offered support for those who wanted help in completing their tax forms accurately. None of those messages produced any measurable changes in compliance, but the fourth did. This last message changed behavior by simply highlighting the fact that "more than 90 percent of Minnesota taxpayers pay their full share of taxes every year."

As Richard Thaler and Cass Sunstein summarize in their book *Nudge: Improving Decisions About Health, Wealth and Happiness,* these findings suggests that "some tax payers are more likely to violate the law because of a misperception—plausibly based on the availability of media or other accounts of cheaters—that the level of compliance is pretty low."

Put simply, people do what they think others do. Tell your learners that others are pulling their compliance weight, and they will too.

Use Role Models to Set the Right Standards

As we just discussed, everything you tell your learner sets a bar for their future behavior. If we set the bar too low, by fixating only on what not to do, we shouldn't be surprised when behavior stoops to that bar's height. And yet so many hours of compliance training continue to fixate on worst case scenarios and cartoonish maleficence, as if misconduct is rampant and our training is the thin line between our organizations and anarchy. If we aren't careful, our learners may take the wrong cue from such learning, and set about living up to the awful standards we've spent so much time depicting.

Instead, we should shift our focus from the lowest common denominator to the highest. We should celebrate our ethical champions, and craft training programs that value and support our best employees, instead of wasting everyone's time and insulting their judgment in a vain attempt to reform a few bad actors.

Bystander intervention, for example, is one of the most effective forms of training for preventing harassment and discrimination. Instead of focusing attention on sensationalized cases of terrible misconduct—perhaps creating the dangerous perception that such conduct is expected at your organization—bystander-based training celebrates the ethical majority of your audience (who would never engage in such behavior) and equips them with the skills they need to sustain the safe and equitable environment they want. Such training sets the right standard, and reinforces the kind of organization your organization actually expects itself to be.

Deputize and Distribute

Knowing that people notice their peers and respond to what they see, we should be spending a lot less time thinking about the message our learners hear from us, and a lot more thinking about the messages they hear from one another.

What better way to wield social influence than to make your learning message a social message? Whether you're adding a message board to an online tutorial, creating more opportunities for meaningful peer interactions in your in-person sessions, or creating a social-driven project plan that uses train-the-trainer resources to distribute your message through existing peer networks within your organization, you can benefit greatly from making your message one that is by and for your learners.

The more your learners perceive ethics and compliance as peer-driven efforts—instead of another hierarchical initiative from some distant (literally or figuratively) company headquarters—the more likely they will be to listen to the message, and to change.

From Context to Habit

By using social influence, affect, and availability to influence our learners' context, we can do more than transfer knowledge or win positive feedback on our post-course surveys. We can reprogram the human machine by strategically altering the most persuasive aspects of its context, making the right course of action as instinctive as eating when you're hungry or pausing when you sense danger.

By designing for context, we can stop misconduct before it has a chance to occur, without wasting too much of our learners' willpower or conscious effort along the way. We can build learning that games the rules of System 1, and changes behavior at its source.

But small changes in context only work when behaviors are flexible and genuine choices are still being made. If choice has already been replaced by habit, good instructional designers have to shift from their role as an architect of context and become an engineer of the habit itself, which we'll explore in the next chapter.

Chapter 8
Making a Habit of Compliance

On a dark Saturday in September 2017, Hurricane Irma surged through Miami Beach. Streets flooded, construction cranes toppled, and 130 mph winds threatened walls, roofs, and trees across the city. Spin-off tornados materialized and vanished on the beach, spitting sand from the ocean to the sky. And through it all—shirtless, in a black headband and a pair of worn sneakers—a 67-year-old man went for his afternoon jog.

Three months earlier, the citizens of Atlanta, Georgia, woke to a pristine Fourth of July holiday, with light cloud cover and a refreshing breeze. Sixty thousand of them had paid the registration fee for the famous Peachtree Road Race, the largest 10k run in the world. They had been planning to run the race for months and had invested their registration fees in the goal. They knew they would be given free water, snacks, and beer; be entertained along the route with live music and fireworks; and receive a commemorative T-shirt for finishing. The weather was ideal, and they would be supported with all the amenities a runner could ask for. And yet, on the morning of the event, more than 5,000 registered runners didn't even bother to show up.

And so, Robert "Raven" Craft ran eight miles through a Miami hurricane for apparently no reason at all, while 5,000 others couldn't muster a mere six miles on a perfect Saturday morning, despite a range of economic incentives and an event that had been laid out to make their run as enjoyable and effortless as possible. You may be tempted to ascribe the difference between these runners to willpower, grit, or determination. But none of those concepts truly explains the stark difference in behavior on those two mornings. Raven showed up for his run because he'd been doing so every single day since 1975, and the Peachtree racers didn't show up for theirs because they hadn't. The difference, as is so often the case, was habit.

Traditional economists, compliance experts, and instructional designers ascribe too much weight to traditional carrot-and-stick models of human behavior. We seem to believe that adults are inherently rational creatures, who simply tally up the incentives in any given situation and make the choice with the most value and the lowest cost. If we want people to quit engaging in a given behavior, we only need to dial up the penalty or dial up the reward for its alternative. Compliance would be easy in such a world, requiring only the right combination of policies. Unfortunately, that isn't the world we live in.

Raven had nothing to gain from his hurricane run in any traditional economic sense. In fact, by sticking to his routine in the face of citywide evacuation orders, his choice to run could be seen as fundamentally irrational, and not at all in his own best interest. The Peachtree skippers, on the other hand, had more than a T-shirt and some free snacks on the line. They'd each paid at least $80 in advance for a spot—$80 that they would have to acknowledge as a pure loss if they failed to participate—and had likely informed friends and family of their intention to run. Not running, in their case, carried real financial and reputational costs, poorly balanced by the benefit of a couple extra hours sleep. If human beings were purely rational, as carrot-and-stick models suggest, you'd expect at least a few of those 5,000 people to have made a different calculation. But we aren't.

In addition to automated reactions based on minor fluctuations in context—which we discussed in the last chapter—most of the rest of human behavior is determined by simple habit. We don't do what we do because it makes sense, or even because we want to do it. We do what we do, most of the time, because it's what we've always done.

These habits, as we've already seen, can be a force for good or evil. If we can learn to understand them—and the factors in their life cycle that we can influence through training—we can stop misconduct that has settled into the daily patterns of our organization and establish new patterns that make the right behaviors much more difficult to avoid.

The Life of a Habit

In his book, *The Power of Habit: Why We Do What We Do in Life and Business,* Charles Duhigg paints a vivid picture of humanity's stubborn habit of forming and keeping habits.

When we encounter a common trigger, which Duhigg calls a cue, we typically react the same way we did the last time we saw that cue, provided our behavior was rewarded and not punished the last time we tried it. If the reward for the behavior is stable over time, the behavior becomes a routine. The result is an entrenched cue-routine-reward cycle, which is what we commonly call a habit.

For example, you probably brushed your teeth this morning. For some, the cue to brush is turning off the alarm and getting up from bed, for others it's getting out of the shower, for others it's finishing breakfast; but whatever your specific cue, you likely brushed your teeth at roughly the same point this morning as you did yesterday and the day before, always in response to the same basic sequence of events. On all those days, you received a reward for your routine: that clean, fresh feeling of a brushed mouth, ready for another day (Exhibit 8-1). And that reward sends you down the same path again tomorrow, and the day after that, forever.

Exhibit 8-1. Cue-Routine-Reward Cycle of Habit

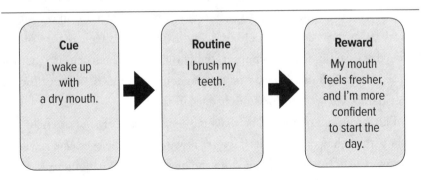

If your normal morning cues are interrupted—perhaps by a crying, four-month-old baby—the new cues may fail to trigger your normal routine and you may forget to brush. If so, you will probably miss your accustomed reward all day, lamenting the film on your teeth, the heaviness of your tongue, and the self-conscious feeling of a neglected mouth. If you suffered such a morning this morning, don't despair. Habits are resilient, and you will almost certainly be back to brushing your teeth tomorrow.

If you want to change a habit for good, you'll need much more than a single interruption. You'll need a new habit to take its place.

Origin of the Teeth Brushing Habit

Your habit of brushing your teeth is no accident. Toothpaste was a rarity in American homes in the early 1900s, until Claud Hopkins bought Peposent toothpaste and used his intuitive understanding of human habit to launch one of the most successful marketing campaigns of all time. He taught consumers to recognize a cue they had previously ignored—the feeling of film on their teeth in the morning—and associated it with an unheard of routine that promised a new reward. He showed how a few minutes of brushing with his toothpaste would leave the mouth feeling fresh in a way that his customers had never known before, and leave their teeth whiter too! A habit was born from those advertisements—a habit that now sells more than 2 billion dollars of toothpaste in the United States every year.

Forming and Breaking Habits

When we encounter a new cue for the first time, we have no habit to fall back on and our minds have to choose an untested behavior in response. In rare cases, that choice is deliberate, willful, and strategic. More often, as we discussed in the last chapter, the choice is a subconscious reaction to the most available aspects of our current context, or a recycling of other habits we've used for similar cues in the past.

Either way, our minds will be watching—subconsciously, but carefully—to see how the behavior pans out. If we are rewarded for the behavior, it will be filed away as a routine and called up the next time we encounter the same cue. If we are punished, or simply fail to receive the reward we anticipated, we'll hopefully learn from that experience and try something new the next time we find ourselves in the same situation. For example, if our initial response to the cue of a boiling kettle is to grab it by its base, the reward of a burnt hand should ensure that behavior doesn't become a habit, and will hopefully have us reaching for the handle next time.

Rewarded behaviors almost always become habit, provided we encounter the same cue often enough for it to be remembered and that other habits don't get in the way. These are the three criteria for a new habit to stick:

- The cue has to recur consistently in situations that allow execution of the same routine.
- The routine has to consistently reap a net-positive reward.
- The routine can't directly conflict with a more deeply entrenched cue-routine-reward cycle.

For example, you may feel good after going to the gym on your way to work one morning, but that reward may not be enough to guarantee a healthy new habit. If you also feel good after sleeping in, your long-entrenched sleep habit might reassert itself before your gym habit has a chance to stick. If you often forget to set your alarm, the lack of a consistent cue will also make it less likely that your sporadic trips to the gym ever become anything resembling an actual habit.

If we want to start, stop, or change a habit, we have to intervene effectively at one or more of these three critical junctures. In some cases, we can create a new cue, eliminate an old cue, or help our learners recognize an existing cue that is often ignored. In other cases, we can make our learners more aware of the internal and external rewards of ethical behavior, or eliminate the lesser rewards they stand to gain from negligent behavior or misconduct. Finally, in some cases, we can highjack entrenched habit loops by keeping the existing cues and rewards, and simply replacing the behavior that comes between. If another routine could generate the same results—more efficiently, effectively, or ethically—we have a chance of winning our learners over to that new routine with old-fashioned skills training techniques, provided the new routine isn't too burdensome and that our learners buy in to the need for change.

The remainder of this chapter will explore tips and opportunities for intervening at each of these three milestones, allowing instructional designers to deconstruct our learners' habits and rebuild them in a form that reduces risk and maximizes compliance.

The Loss Aversion Principle

As we discussed in the last chapter, the average person values losses roughly twice as heavily as they value gains. Sometimes referred to as the psychological law of inertia, this overvaluing of potential losses causes many to refrain from even rational changes, as their fear of what they stand to lose from the change outshines any hope for what they may stand to gain. If you expect to change your learner's habits, you must do everything you can to combat this impulse by dialing up the rewards of the new habit and assuaging any fears your learners have over what they are giving up. Change is possible; the reasons just have to be especially compelling.

Changing Cues

We live in cue-rich environments. Our senses are continuously assaulted by signs and signifiers that seek to win our attention and influence our actions, far more than we could ever consciously notice. On a single drive to work, our attention is demanded by traffic lights, billboards, the brake lights of other drivers, radio advertisements, chit chat from our passengers, and our own internal monologue of regrets, daydreams, and to-dos.

With demand high and attention scarce, direct habitual cues are often our most reliable avenue for influencing behavior. But to succeed, we need to find and champion cues that can consistently capture our learner's attention, even through all that daily noise. Surprisingly, and luckily, the most effective cues don't always require a massive marketing budget or constant handholding. In fact, the best cues are often quite simple.

For example, the cue of a tiny etched fly in a urinal has been shown to decrease spillage rates in airport bathrooms by up to 80 percent, as attested by a very happy facilities manager at Schiphol Airport in Amsterdam, where the fly etchings were introduced in an effort to improve men's aim while using the bathroom. The success led to similar etchings and stickers in busy bathrooms across the world. The case study is usually cited as evidence for the power of attention and focus, but it works equally well as an illustration of habit. The cue of the fly—a clear, attention-grabbing target—triggers the routine of aiming, and the intrinsic reward of hitting one's target (Exhibit 8-2). You may think men would extract a similar reward from landing every drop in any urinal, but without the clear cue of the fly, the aiming routine often fails to trigger, much to the dismay of angry janitors across the globe.

Exhibit 8-2. How Changing a Cue Can Create the Habit of Marksmanship

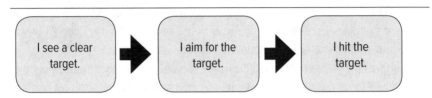

The right cue, presented in the right moment, can trigger dramatic differences in behavior. If we hope to reduce misconduct and increase compliance, we need to use our training to create lasting cues that help our employees direct their attention where it's most needed.

For example, a compliance team could create a training program that helps learners recognize the feeling of discomfort they experience when asked to do something they feel is wrong. Competing corporate priorities may have taught many employees to ignore those cues in the past, but they likely still exist within your learners, and can be resurfaced with tools like storytelling, reflection, and physiological associations. If learners recognize the presence of an ethical dilemma the next time they feel sweaty and uncomfortable, you can train them to engage in any number of behaviors in response—like calling your ethics advisor, consulting your policy library, or creating an anonymous ethics reporting ticket. Those behaviors are fairly easy to train and likely to be replicated in the moment of need, provided you can draw your learners' attention to the initial cue.

Tips for Leveraging Cues

Before we can change our learners' routines, we need to get their attention. The following tips can help you craft the kind of cues that spark lasting new habits.

Embedded Training

Instructional designers have long known that training becomes far more effective the closer it moves to the moment of need. This has led to a rise in embedded, just-in-time training for key business drivers like customer service, sales, and safety. You can leverage the same principles in compliance to ensure your learners encounter cues for ethical behavior at the moment they most need to see them.

For example, instead of making managers sit through training on recruitment bias and diversity hiring practices when they are first promoted to the role, why not wait and have them take the training when they add their first requisition to your hiring system? The message will seem much more relevant if it arrives when they are in a position to use it, and even if they don't learn anything new from your course, the timing of the message might cue a more responsible routine. Perhaps you can even make a refresher version of the course—one that's short and highly focused—for managers to complete every time they launch a new hiring process. Even if it's only a single question and a 30 second piece of media, that microlearning can become a useful, habituated cue that alters real hiring practices at your organization.

Pre-Attestations

When adult learners see the familiar cue of another check-the-box compliance course—including a legal sounding title, abstract objectives, an emphasis on requirements over values, and other branding missteps that we will discuss in a later chapter—those cues trigger the familiar routine of click-through-this-as-quickly-as-possible. If you want to trigger real, transformative learning, you need to start your training with better cues.

For example, if your course features a post-learning attestation where learners pledge to honor the policies you just discussed and preserve the values of the organization, consider moving that attestation to the front of the course instead. By asking your learners to vouch for their commitment to what they are about to learn, you may cue routines like attentive reading, critical reflection, ownership, and intentionality, all of which will make your content far more likely to stick.

Notes to Self

Self-generated cues—like the clichéd string around the finger—can be useful for triggering the routines your learners want to remember. Consider offering postage-paid postcards that your learners can use to write messages to themselves during your training. Then you can collect them and mail them back to the participants a few weeks later as a reminder of their intentions.

Websites like futureme.org allow learners to craft short emails to themselves that the server will store and mail back a year later. If the cue from the past arrives at the right moment, it may trigger the preferred routine, generate the intrinsic reward of following through on a self-defined goal, and re-establish better habits that permanently reduce risk at your organization.

Reinforcement

A great training course may cue your learners to try new behaviors immediately after class, but those routines will soon fade if the cue is never encountered again. If you want your training to be the cue that changes your learners' behavior, you have to get that content back in front of them as often as possible. Microlearning and continuous communication campaigns, as we discussed in the last chapter, are far better tools for cultivating habit than a single annual tutorial ever could be.

Changing Routines

We don't always need to add or change cues to change behavior. If we can identify the cues that already command our learners' attention, we can hijack those existing signals and tie them to more desirable reactions. In other words, we can keep the cue and the reward, but change the routine that connects them.

To understand how this might work in the compliance space, it pays to take a deeper view of habit and behavior. Instead of specific routines—like smoking when you have a break or getting a coffee when you are tired—much of our daily behavior can be attributed to more generalized habits, or ways of reacting, to the vast sea of cues that confront us every day. These patterns of behavior resurface in our lives again and again, defining the kind of people we are and the kinds of organizations we build together.

For example, some organizations prioritize speed and productivity above all else, with an occasional safety presentation for good measure. Other organizations put safety first in everything they do, with an emphasis on doing things the right way and an assumption that productivity will follow. That might seem like a small difference in perspective, but the values each organization prioritizes and reinforces will likely influence countless smaller habits within their employee base, offering a template response that can be repeated each time an employee is forced to decide between doing what's quick and doing what's right. If you visit a construction site where employees forget to wear safety vests when riding a scissor lift, you can be sure that other safety violations are happening elsewhere on the site. The lack of vest is actually a sub-habit—a symptom of a broader behavioral blueprint.

These recurring, universal habits are perpetuated by the same basic principles as the other habits we've discussed; their rewards just apply to a broader range of cues and routines. A majority of misconduct, for example, can be attributed to a modern human habit that often serves us well, but goes terribly wrong when it doesn't: the path of least resistance.

People are busy. We are faced with constant competing priorities, and challenging circumstances that never stop shifting. Fires must be found and extinguished quickly, because a new fire is already sparking to life across the hall. To function in this demanding world, we have grown very adept at spotting and following the path of least resistance in almost any scenario. And that aptitude has become a defining habit for many modern organizations.

Whenever an employee's status quo is interrupted—by a new item that needs to be purchased, a new seat on their team that needs to be filled, or a new demand from a manager or request from a customer—that employee will probably find and take the path of least resistance to the only real reward we've taught them to expect in many business settings: a brief sense of accomplishment, and a momentary return to the comfort of their status quo (Exhibit 8-3).

Exhibit 8-3. Making Compliance the Path of Least Resistance

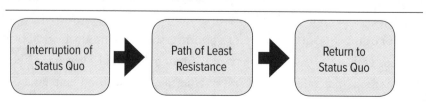

In our fervent rush from interruption back to status quo, we might bend or ignore procurement laws, hire the most readily available candidate instead of striving to find the most qualified, and prioritize speed and ease in meeting new requests, instead of long-term values like safety, security, and fairness. If a value or policy isn't clearly marked along the path of least resistance, we'll usually get where we're going without even noticing it on the map.

If we want to change behavior on the largest possible scale, we have to change the paths of least resistance at our organizations. Luckily, as instructional designers, we are experts at charting paths that our employees can follow, and we can apply the same proven skills we've used in technical training fields to help our employees master and retain routines that are more consistently in line with our organizations' policies and values.

The Many Habits of a Model Employee

Your employees engage in countless habits in any given day, and those habits can make the difference between misconduct and better ethical decisions. Your training can achieve dramatic behavioral results by creating the right kind of habits and making them easy to keep.

Specific Behaviors

When you've identified a required routine in response to a specific cue—like how to safely operate a forklift, or how to handle customer data after taking a credit card payment—use simulations and assessments to drill the preferred routines into the minds and muscle-memory of the relevant audiences. With practice and clear instructions, a well-trained routine will be the first to surface the next time your employee encounters the expected cue, especially if you reinforce the training regularly until the habit is firmly entrenched.

As an added training tool, consider helping your employees craft their own plans for how they will maintain the routine, and how they will react to any expected obstacles.

Finding and Following Instructions

Good instructions can make anything easier, and a simple library of job aids and quick guides can become the kind of resource that redefines the path of least resistance at your organization. But only if your employees make a habit of using it.

Instead of teaching a specific routine for every possible cue—a daunting task, to say the least—create an easy-to-follow guide for every routine and teach your employees to use those guides. Just make sure your resource library has answers to the most likely questions, and that those answers are accurate and easy to find. If not, your learners may not get any reward from your library, and returning will never become a habit.

Seeking Help and Guidance

Conduct can be complex, and the right decision in many situations may require professional guidance. If your organization has invested in such support tools—like ethics officers, hotlines, employee assistance programs, or specialized advisors for complex issues like sexual harassment or cyber security—your training should seek to establish the habit of using them. The general habit, "when in doubt, ask," can be reinforced through your training and communications as the preferred response to common cues like discomfort, anxiety, or confusion. If you can make those channels easy to access and likely to achieve rewards—which we will discuss next—you can spawn an overarching habit that reduces all forms of misconduct at your organization.

Changing Rewards

Just because we put a new path in front of our audience, there is no guarantee they will take it. We can increase our chances by making the right paths easier to follow, as we just discussed, but even lateral changes take some effort, and our learners won't allocate that effort if they don't feel the incentive.

As instructional designers, we may think that we don't have much control over which behaviors are rewarded or punished within our organizations. Raises, promotions, and disciplinary action are the purview of managers and senior leadership, and those business leaders don't often stop to seek input from learning and development. If we can't change the rewards that hit our employees' wallets, how can we hope to change habits? Perhaps by broadening our understanding of what counts as a reward.

Recent sociological and business research suggest that traditional carrot and stick incentives only account for a portion of our employees' motivation and decision making. In fact, a famous meta-analysis of more than 128 studies conducted by Edward Deci and associates (1999) found that extrinsic incentives aren't the most effective rewards for influencing performance, and they may even be counter-productive. Instead, we can achieve far better results by building motivation though our employees' intrinsic incentives—

like challenge, purpose, and autonomy—which we'll discuss further in the next chapter.

Most people aren't consciously and continuously calculating their decisions to maximize their financial returns. We may occasionally scheme, connive, or engage in strategic acts of blatant self-promotion, but we're usually too busy to be that clever. Instead, many of our decisions in the workplace are made with one of two rewards in mind, at least subconsciously:

- **The internal satisfaction of doing what's right.** Our employees sometimes need learning and support to make the best possible decisions, but they do not need to be taught to be ethical. A 2007 study by Felix Warneken and Michael Tomasello revealed that children as young as 14 months will act on an intrinsic human desire to help others, and even the most hardened corporate professional can likely think of several decisions a day made for no grander reason than a simple desire to do what's right. Interestingly, a subsequent study by Warneken and Tomasello (2008) found that the introduction of extrinsic rewards can actually reduce the likelihood of helping behavior among 20-month-old babies, suggesting that while our intrinsic motivation to help is present from infancy, so too is our complicated love/hate relationship with external incentives.

- **The relief of returning to the status quo.** As we've already discussed, the habit at the source of many instances of misconduct is a too-hasty return to our comfortable status quo, taken along the path of least resistance. There is immediate satisfaction in solving problems and resolving needs, even if the resolution reached is less than ideal.

Many, if not most, of your daily habits are likely correlated to one of these two fundamental rewards, and nothing more. You hold the door open for a stranger walking into work behind you, you wash the dishes, you help a child with their homework—none of these actions come with a tangible reward, except the feeling you get from doing good. You eat snacks in the evening not because you're hungry, but because it's what you do in the evening while sitting in front of the TV. The reward for the habit is the perpetuation of the habit itself, and the comfortable status quo it helps you maintain.

While human nature is much more complex than a pursuit of these two simple rewards, the relationship between these two fundamental drivers provides a useful simplification for compliance training purposes. It's productive to assume that a significant portion of corporate misconduct occurs when imperfect habits are consistently rewarded with a satisfying return to status quo, never allowing more appropriate habits to achieve deeper rewards and flourish.

For example, imagine a web designer. It's fair to assume, even without having met, that this web designer cares about other human beings, at least at some level, and would not deliberately seek to persecute or exclude others in her daily life. However, if this web designer has a huge workload and limited resources, she may opt to neglect accessibility requirements in her haste to meet her manager's demands. This is especially true if her manager has always accepted nonaccessible deliverables without question in the past. If the desired reward is only a happy manager and a finished project—and it often is—then the web designer may find herself embracing habits that simply get the project off her desk, without even noticing that she could be doing more to make her application fair, effective, and universally accessible. Instead of achieving a greater good, she has only maintained the status quo.

This does not mean that people are unethical. If you asked your employees which they would rather do—what is right, or what is easy—very few would answer with the latter. The problem is that organizations don't ask the question often enough. Worse still, they craft environments that subvert employees' best intentions by asking them to blindly follow policies and unwritten expectations without question or deviation, effectively robbing them of their ethical agency and taking away the intrinsic reward of doing what's right for the sake of doing what's right. The result, unsurprisingly, is misconduct.

If we can remind our employees what ethical satisfaction at work feels like, we can use that deeper reward to drive them away from misconduct and toward more appropriate routines. We simply have to replace our message of "do this, or you will be fired," with the message "do this, because you know it's right." The first message only reinforces the reward of the status quo; the second hints at a higher calling.

This approach is on full display in Starbucks's much-publicized approach to diversity training in 2018 following a high-profile case of racial profiling and hyper-policing at one of their stores. The content released to the public after the event made no mention of disciplinary action or dogmatic policies, but instead focused a documentarian's eye on the experience of race in the United States, and the role that responsible Starbucks employees can and should play in championing inclusivity. The program reminded Starbucks employees to feel proud of the value they provide as a common gathering space in diverse communities, instead of just feeling compelled to follow some new policy in an effort not to get caught in the next scandal.

Altering rewards doesn't require any added budget, executive buy-in, or wholesale revisions in the way we manage performance. It simply requires that we align our training with the real values and internal rewards that our employees are seeking anyway, instead of the rigid stipulations and threats that have defined so many compliance policies and training programs in the past. If we want our employees to follow our lead, they have to believe we're headed someplace they actually want to be, and they have to believe we'll get there.

Tips for Changing Rewards Through Training

Change is never anyone's first option. Our job, as compliance experts and instructional designers, is to find and spotlight the most compelling reasons for change. If we can alter the reward that looms largest in our learners' minds when the cue is encountered, we can change their behavior.

Make the Invisible Visible

The example of the accessible website we discussed earlier illustrates another problematic issue with the way our brains subconsciously assess rewards. We tend to prioritize rewards that are immediate, visceral, and in close proximity, while ignoring rewards that are abstract or distant from us in time and place. As a result, we may choose the path that most quickly satisfies the manager standing over our desk, without even thinking about the long-term consequences of an accessibility law we may be circumventing, or the unfair impact our shortcut may have on a future user who is unable to access our services.

Many compliance tutorials seek to redress issues like this with an appeal to statistics or more laws, but those abstract concerns will never compete with the urgency of our learners' immediate incentives and disincentives. Instead, you need to make the need for accessibility feel near, real, and present. You need to become an expert storyteller.

A compelling story of an individual personally affected by an inaccessible website can do more to change behavior than 100 policies or laws. It reminds your learners of the real value of their actions, and allows them to aim their habits at a higher reward than mere compliance.

For example, I was once part of an instructional design consortium that invited a blind member of our community to demonstrate how he used screen readers to navigate his computer and complete his daily work. He showed us how easy it was for him to move through an accessible website, and how impossible it was to move through a site where even a few accessibility requirements had been skipped. While I'd always been aware of accessibility requirements for e-learning—508(c) for example—I was only making the most cursory allowances for accessibility. After one hour with an effected user, however, accessibility has become a central driver as I'm developing programs. Once distant and abstract, how blind or deaf users will experience my work is now a constant concern. I am more comfortable pushing back when a customer asks me to speed up a project by skipping closed-captioning, and I look for new solutions that do more than meet the letter of the law, but that can actually make the program as universally accessible as possible. That is the power of a real, human story to reshape the rewards that guide our actions.

Train Peers, Customers, Managers, and Internal Auditors

If the primary audience you need to reach is too busy or too set in their old habits to hear your pitch for a deeper reward, consider targeting your training on the environment around them instead. If you inspire the community to raise their expectations and demand change, you can change the conditions under which the status quo can be achieved. If the quick and dirty solution no longer appeases your learners' primary stakeholders or peers, their incentive to change becomes much stronger.

Think of the sign at the grocery store check-out that says, "If your attendant doesn't offer a receipt, you can enjoy a soda on us." This is a more effective model for behavior change than simply adding more mandatory training for the cashiers. The threat of that awkward conversation with a customer, and the effort of filling out the form for the lost soda, makes handing over a receipt suddenly feel like the easiest option.

If the path of least resistance in your compliance subject leads to an undesirable but often accepted outcome, you can educate your community—peers, managers, customers, and policy holders—to make that outcome less acceptable. By removing the most common reward for misconduct—a return to the status quo—you can prime your audience to embrace a new routine.

Train First-Line Responders

If your training program encourages your learners to reach out for professional support when the right course of action is unclear, make sure those professionals are trained to provide sufficiently rewarding responses. Your training should prepare your responders to anticipate the most common issues and readily offer a solution that legally and ethically meets real business needs. If your responders can provide such solutions—while also reinforcing your learners' core values by thanking them for seeking help—that response will go a long way toward establishing a lasting habit. If the call is less pleasant or productive, the routine of reaching out for guidance is less likely to be triggered next time.

Thank Your Learners

Thank your learners for their commitment and values as often as possible during your training. These simple gestures can help reinforce your learners' innate desire to do what's right, reminding them to feel good about doing good. If you can build thank you messages into your real world processes—like an automated accessibility checker that sends a congratulatory email to a site owner when the site passes a 508(c) audit—that feedback can make it easier for your learners to associate their behavior with its deeper rewards, and make it more likely to stick as a routine.

A Final Note in Defense of Humanity

The last two chapters painted a somewhat pessimistic view of humanity. If we aren't blindly following the whims of our context and the peer pressure of those around us like lemmings, we're blindly following the same patterns we have in the past, for no better reasons than stubbornness, laziness, and resistance to change.

Pessimistic or not, we are often creatures of context and habit. Recognizing that truth can do more than anything else to increase the behavioral effectiveness of our training. The GDPR Habit Plan presented in appendix 3 shows how easy it can be to solve behavioral problems once we stop targeting our compliance training at the law or the learner's sense of reason, and start targeting the habits themselves.

This does not mean, however, that our employees are mindless automatons. People engage in wondrous acts of heroism, courage, and free will every day. We may follow our context and habits often, but we can also transcend them. We can be creative and spontaneous, capable of nearly any feat we set our minds to achieving. We only have to put our sights on a good target. And for that, we have to be motivated.

The next chapter will explore the somewhat counterintuitive methods that can spark such motivation. If successful, the internal drive of our learners can change the way we approach compliance and learning completely, making context and habit far less consequential and our desired behavior changes much more robust, comprehensive, and resilient.

But before we unleash our army of motivated, independent employee philosophers, we should remember that the right set of simple habits—easy to teach and easily repeatable—can often reap the same rewards. Sometimes, if you want to change the world, you only need to change its habits.

Chapter 9

Intrinsic Motivation and the Thrill of Problem-Based Learning

Daniel Pink begins his book *Drive: The Surprising Truth About What Motivates Us* with the story of two simple studies that should change the way economists and organizations consider human behavior. They should also change the way we think about compliance training.

In the first story, Professor Harry F. Harlow and his colleagues at the University of Wisconsin set out to measure the ability of rhesus monkeys to solve complex problems. The researchers devised clever mechanical puzzles that the monkeys would have to solve to unlock a small food compartment that hid a delicious treat. They'd planned a two-week study, measuring whether the monkeys could learn to solve the puzzles more quickly and reliably after being conditioned by the rewards. But the monkeys had a faster timetable in mind.

Before the researchers had a chance to place any food inside the puzzles, the monkeys began playing with the interesting new contraptions. They seemed to recognize the puzzles in their cages, immediately, as a problem to be solved. And apparently, monkeys like solving problems.

"Unbidden by any outside urging and unprompted by the experimenters," Pink notes, "the monkeys began playing with the puzzles with focus, determination, and what looked like enjoyment. And in short order, they began figuring out how the contraptions worked. By the time Harlow tested the monkeys on days 13 and 14 of the experiment, the primates had become quite adept. They solved the puzzles frequently and quickly; two-thirds of the time they cracked the code in less than sixty seconds."

The monkeys accomplished those excellent learning outcomes without any formal training and without the promise of any external reward. At the time, most scientists believed that all animal behavior was driven either by fundamental biological urges—like sleeping when tired, or eating when hungry—or by conditioned responses to the rewards and punishments present in their environment. For example, a monkey could learn not to touch a fence that delivered a shock or to push a button that delivered a treat. But the monkeys in Harlow's study weren't conditioned to solve the puzzles at all. They had nothing to gain from the experience—except the intrinsic motivation of solving the puzzle itself.

Even more shocking to the classical behaviorists, the introduction of food to the puzzles actually diminished the results! Perhaps, in human parlance, the addition of a paid incentive made it feel too much like a job. The task became less interesting and enjoyable, and instead began to feel like another clinical test, another rote task, another research box to check. It lost the thrill of just being a problem to solve, and learning suffered as a result.

The second study, conducted by Edward Deci, confirmed that this powerful intrinsic drive was not reserved only for monkeys. Humans enjoy solving problems, too. When given a choice between playing with a set of Soma puzzle pieces or taking a break and reading a magazine, participants in Deci's study who had previously been paid for solving puzzles quickly lost interest in the puzzles and shifted their attention to the magazines. However, those who had never been paid—who had only ever solved puzzles for the sake of solving the puzzles—remained much more focused and determined to achieve better results, sometimes even staying at the table and testing new combinations long after the experiment itself had ended!

In the previous two chapters, we discussed human beings as if they were simple machines. We explored how changes in context could condition different responses, or how subtle changes in cues, routines, and rewards could create new habits. While these different methods can be powerful, they are not the full picture of human behavior. There is a third lever that, if wielded effectively, can be the most transformative learning tool of all: intrinsic motivation.

Human beings are not, after all, just machines. If we give our employees the chance, they can show themselves to be so much more.

Intrinsic Motivation and Compliance

In the last chapter, we explored how we can change the reward calculations that determine our learner's habits without promising raises, promotions, or other financial incentives. We don't need such rewards, or the looming threat of punishment, to get our learners' attention. In fact, there is good reason to believe that such incentives can be counterproductive.

In their book *Primed to Perform: How to Build the Highest Performing Cultures Through the Science of Total Motivation*, authors Neel Doshi and Lindsay McGregor use a library of business case studies to advance a similar message to that of Harlow, Deci, and Pink. In their summary of "total motivation," they offer a useful inventory of the kinds of extrinsic motivators that corporations too often wield to their own detriment. These imperfect motivators include:

- **Emotional pressure.** Employees do what they do because they are made to feel guilty if they don't. (Workplace examples: passive aggressive emails and public shaming reports.)
- **Economic Pressure.** Employees do what they do for fear of losing their job, money, or livelihood. (Workplace example: direct threats of disciplinary action.)
- **Inertia.** Employees do what they do because it's what they've always done. (Workplace examples: unspoken expectations, unexamined routines, unexplained directives, and the unquestioned status quo.)

These incentives are everywhere in the modern organization, but they aren't nearly as resilient as intrinsic rewards, or as powerful. As Doshi remarked to a recent gathering of ethics and compliance experts, "Imagine the motivations a couple might have for getting and staying married. If the only reasons they can cite for staying married are these three extrinsic motivators—I'd feel guilty if I left, I can't afford to leave, or I haven't really had time to think about leaving—that might be enough to keep them married, at least for a while longer. But that doesn't mean they don't have a problem."

Extrinsic motivators offer a dangerous illusion of unity and shared purpose that may not actually exist. A robust set of extrinsic motivators may make an organization appear stronger and more accountable, but a sole reliance on external rewards can make our employees less adaptive, less resilient, and more vulnerable to future misconduct. Unfortunately, traditional compliance training is rife with extrinsic motivation.

When we focus our tutorials, courses, and policies on rules and incentives—what you can't do, what you must do, and what will happen to you if you don't comply—we rob our learners of their ethical agency and rob our subjects of their intrinsic value. Just like the human and monkey puzzle-solvers we encountered at the beginning of this chapter, such external incentives only serve to cheapen the intrinsic appeal of the problem itself, and distract from the natural desire to do good for the sake of doing good. The result is less determined, creative, purposeful learning, and more going through the motions.

Luckily, the work of Pink, Doshi, and McGregor also offer a detailed survey of the sounder ground our future training offerings should build on. Their books provide countless tips on how to leverage the superior, intrinsic motivators that businesses have too often neglected in the past, defined by concepts like autonomy, mastery, purpose, play, and potential. For our purposes, we will adopt an even simpler definition: To foster intrinsically motivated learning and create lasting change, we have to give our learners a genuine problem to solve, and we have to let them solve it.

Problem-Based Learning

Problem-based learning (PBL) became a reputable and often-studied pedagogical framework after the work of Howard Barrows and Robyn Tamblyn at McMaster University, including their original book on the method, *Problem-Based Learning: An Approach to Medical Education.* As the authors state in this seminal text, the PBL approach was crafted in response to several known ills within traditional academic models, including a lack of intrinsic motivation among students and a lack of contextualized learning outcomes. Traditional, definition-heavy medical education was making learning less likely to occur, and less likely to transfer to the real world when it did.

As the authors state in the introductory chapter of their text, "A student's acquisition of a large body of knowledge in medicine and the basic sciences is no assurance that he knows when or how to apply this knowledge in the care of patients" (Barrows and Tamblyn 1980). Similarly, a compliance learner's ability to click through slides or pass definition-heavy quizzes is not likely to make them better decision makers or increase the odds of compliant behavior back in the workplace.

Motivated by the potentially life-threatening outcomes of poor medical training, Barrows and Tamblyn set out to find a more reliable approach to learning. They came to believe it was more important for a medical school to teach its students how to think through challenging problems than to teach a subject-based curriculum of facts and theories. Facts have limited scope and a tendency to change, after all, while an ability to think and reason offers endless value.

Facts and definitions are still important, in medicine and in compliance, and the PBL program at McMaster University did not intend to let students graduate without core knowledge of basic scientific principles. Instead, they kept the traditions of the academic classroom—where content is explained, demonstrated, and applied—and flipped the order to mimic the process by which we learn and grow in the real world. The genius of problem-based learning, as Barrows and Tamblyn indicate with enthusiasm, is that "The problem is encountered first in the learning process!"

By opening with a challenging, real-world, multidisciplinary problem, the learners can quickly assess what they already know, what they need to know, and why this knowledge is important. A good problem, question, or puzzle inspires the learners' intrinsic motivation to learn and triggers the natural human desire to move from problems to solutions. In the process, PBL aims to promote "the acquisition of an integrated body of knowledge related to the problem, and the development or application of problem-solving skills" (Barrows and Tamblyn 1980). Wouldn't those be positive outcomes for your next compliance program?

Common PBL Characteristics

There are six common characteristics of problem-based learning.

Learning Starts With the Problem
PBL experiences always begin with the introduction of a relevant and challenging problem. All content is provided only in the context of solving the problem.

Ill-Structured Problems
Instead of organizing content around topics and subjects, the training program is structured around complex problems that require the integration of key skills and knowledge across a range of subjects.

Resource-Rich Environments
Ample resources, support tools, and scaffolding help learners model effective problem-solving strategies.

Collaborative Learning
Teamwork and social resources are emphasized to facilitate social learning and mirror the real-life collaboration required for solving difficult challenges.

Real-World Techniques
Problems are structured to ensure that the solution requires the skills and knowledge applicable to the learner's role, emphasizing the use of the real behaviors and strategies needed for real-world success.

Self-Ownership
Learners decide what and how they need to learn to solve the problem, and they are given the freedom to fail or reach alternative solutions, just as in real life.

Applying PBL to Compliance
PBL is ideally presented as a holistic curriculum where all learning is guided through the introduction and resolution of progressively difficult

problems, carefully designed to ensure the integration of core subject matter throughout the process. In the strictest models, there is no linear classroom environment or subject-focused lessons. Instead, key subject matter is called up and integrated only in the context of solving each new problem. If the problems are ill-structured enough—requiring key pieces of content from a variety of subjects to reach a successful resolution— then a student's ability to address all the problems assigned throughout an entire curriculum would be enough to demonstrate mastery of all core-required subjects.

Unfortunately, this redefinition of adult learning may not be achievable in every organization, especially to fields as sensitive and traditional as compliance training. Luckily, promising research by Anastasia Elder (2019) at Mississippi State University suggests that many of PBL's benefits can be achieved through brief PBL experiences embedded within traditional learning programs. Elder used a PBL-informed approach to change the structure of a single assignment within a semester-long undergraduate course, and still found that the experience achieved higher levels of student motivation and engagement, even though the structure of the rest of the course and the overarching program remained traditionally academic.

Wherever your compliance learning programs stand today or however resistant your leadership is to change, there are PBL best practices that you could embed in your next project. While each change is relatively small, with minimum impact on the existing design and development process, their outcomes for your learners can be immediate and lasting.

The following five tips form a representative if not exhaustive list of ways PBL may be applied to compliance training. You can select individual tips from this menu to improve learner engagement and learning outcomes within an existing course, or combine all five to build a new experience that reflects the full wisdom of PBL and unleashes your learners' innate motivation to investigate, solve problems, and grow. As a further aid, appendix 4 presents outlines of three sample experiences that apply all five PBL tips to create a problem-based approach for common compliance learning needs.

Tip 1: Start With a Problem

The easiest of the five tips to implement within traditional compliance training is also among the most influential. Too often in the classroom and the online tutorial, relevant case studies and complex scenarios are added as an afterthought to dry content rather than a call to learning. You may have seen this demonstrated in a recent course you attended or designed. It starts out with a list of objectives, then proceeds to explain all the content that was deemed relevant to those objectives by the SME, only to conclude, if the learner is lucky, with a chance for hands-on practice or a problem-solving scenario that hopes to reinforce the content and prompt it to stick.

The commonsense appeal of this structure is dangerous. How can you expect your learners to solve a problem, after all, if you haven't already given them the information they need? If you ask challenging questions before you teach them the answers, aren't you setting them up to fail?

While this reasoning may seem intuitive from a traditional training perspective, modern adult learning theories show that the content-then-exercise approach is deeply flawed. Our number 1 imperative as adult educators must be to engage our learners and inspire their intrinsic motivation to learn. The easiest way to achieve this shift is to flip the order of our courses and programs: Start with a compelling problem that makes the need for training clear and allow the learner to generate their own insights about how prepared or unprepared they are to address that challenge. After giving the learners time to think, try, and digest, debrief the activity with the content required to alleviate any remaining confusion and better prepare the audience to tackle similar problems in the future.

By starting with the problem, you are priming your learners for the content and making them more willing and able to absorb it. This approach is especially effective if the opening problem is genuinely difficult and relevant, which takes us to our second tip.

Tip 2: Add Competing Priorities to Create a Genuine Dilemma

If the solution to your opening problem is immediately apparent to the average learner, then it's not a problem at all. For example, imagine having your audience watch a video scenario of a till operator trying to decide whether or not to pocket a $20 bill. You pause the video before it concludes and ask the audience what they would do in this situation. This exercise suggests a semblance of engagement and interactivity, but the problem is false and its impact on learning is counterproductive. Everyone in the room knows immediately what the right answer should be, and they also know immediately that this training is not going to be interesting or relevant. You've lost their problem-solving motivation from the opening exercise, and it will be extremely difficult to win back.

Instead, your opening problems should be difficult enough to generate real discussion and the possibility of a wrong answer. The best way to ensure this challenge is to search out and add the competing priorities that make real-life choices so much more difficult than they might seem on paper. Instead of the till example, imagine that a cashier in your café is asked by a homeless person whether they have any food to spare. The cashier knows that many unsold sandwiches and sides are thrown out every night, and might be tempted to give $20 worth of food to help the man in need. Would that ever be alright? If so, under what circumstances? Those are much more genuine questions, much more worthy of real problem solving.

Compliant, ethical behavior is easy in a vacuum, but can be extremely challenging to achieve consistently in the real world. By acknowledging and incorporating the real complications that give rise to genuine dilemmas and bad decisions, you can engage your learners' attention and prepare them much more effectively to apply what they've learned in their complex daily lives.

Don't be afraid of the gray area! That's where your learners want your help most, and that's where the opportunities for real learning can be found.

The Ingredients of a Genuine Dilemma

A genuine sense of dilemma can be hard to convey without appearing contrived or fake. Consider the following ingredients when crafting compelling, genuinely challenging compliance scenarios.

Safety vs. Efficiency

How can I balance OSHA requirements and my safety with the need to be productive and finish the job on time?

Personal Accountability vs. Obedience to Authority

When is it insubordinate to tell my manager "no"? When is saying "no" ethically or legally required?

Individual vs. Social Responsibility

When should I act on my concerns for the well-being of others? When should I mind my own business?

Confidentiality vs. Security

What if I have confidential knowledge that might affect others? Should I place a higher weight on the potential impact of my knowledge, or on the requirements for confidentiality?

Customer Service vs. Compliance Restrictions

Can I help a customer by circumventing a policy? What if the customer's need seems more pressing or relevant than the rule?

Strict Adherence vs. Flexibility

How do I know which laws are hard and fast, and which provide room for interpretation?

Stability vs. Progress

Should I go with the flow for the sake of team harmony, or challenge behavior I think is wrong, even if that belief might be subjective?

Tip 3: Allow Learners to Model Real, Relevant Behaviors and Strategies

Whenever possible, format the problem and course structure in a way that mimics your audience's daily reality and allows them to practice the real problem-solving strategies that they will be asked to use in the workplace.

Even high-budget online tutorials too often forget this simple rule. It's admirable to try to engage audiences through the use of a dramatic device—like a slick gameshow-style production, or an espionage thriller parody where the spy encounters key corporate learning objectives en route to thwarting an evil villain—but it's far better to present compelling dilemmas that learners might actually face in the real world. For example, in the initial PBL approach created by Barrows and Tamblyn, nearly every problem started the same way. A patient comes to you, as their doctor, and presents a problem in the form of their symptoms or ailment. The basic format ensures that the experience is relevant to you as an aspiring doctor and allows you to solve problems in the same setting that you will face again and again in your professional life. Instead of creating artificial experiences for the sake of variety or diversion, the details of the patients and their symptoms can be adjusted to provide ample novelty and challenge, and to accommodate nearly any medical learning objective.

This kind of honest, real-life scenario is not only more likely to resonate with your audience, it is also more likely to achieve the desired behavior change beyond the classroom. By choosing problems that require the integration and application of real skills, you allow the learners to model the actual strategies they will need in a safe space. By simulating reality as realistically as possible, your compliance content gains the context required for learning transfer and lasting behavior change.

A dramatic fictional device is rarely necessary to capture your audience's attention. The real problems they face every day are just as interesting, and their solutions can be far more meaningful.

Tip 4: Integrate Multiple Compliance Mandates

It can be difficult to think of compelling real-world problems for 70 separate courses that cover 70 different compliance mandates. But what if you could create 10 great problems that integrate the required and useful points from all 70 subjects?

This is what PBL calls *ill-structured problems*. The interdisciplinary nature of such problems is perfectly suited to complex fields like medicine, where patients don't care if knowledge comes from a biochemistry textbook or a basic anatomy course, as long as it leads to a cure. As the scope of modern compliance mandates becomes more varied and complex, this type of catchall problem may be our salvation too. We shouldn't care whether our employees have memorized all 70 policies; what matters is that they can apply what they need to know to avoid misconduct in the moment of need.

By creating a separate course for each mandate and organizing the courses by compliance subject, we've made it easy to run the reports needed to demonstrate legal compliance. At the same time, we have flooded our learners with redundant or irrelevant courses that address the same few problems over and over with slightly varied terms, requirements, and definitions. We can streamline our offerings and dramatically improve the experience for our learners by structuring our libraries around problems instead. A few good problems can take the place of many separate tutorials by prompting the integration of key content from each subject within the natural process of reaching each solution.

For example, instead of making a new nurse take five different courses that outline the legal requirements for registering a patient, drawing blood, labeling blood, safely handling blood, and protecting patients' data, you could have the new nurse take one course that's based on the real-life problem of processing a patient alone on a busy day. The relevant points from each of the five compliance mandates can be integrated naturally within the flow of the problem, called up by the nurse only when needed during the real-life process.

In this case, the nurse spends an hour exploring and practicing a fundamental aspect of the job instead of spending five hours pretending to learn a series of legal definitions punctuated by repetitive case studies and scenarios. As an added bonus, your instructional design team can focus its efforts on building one hour of great content instead of five hours of mediocre content, demonstrating another way that good compliance training need not entail added budget or resources.

The largest obstacle to this approach is the siloed nature of compliance and subject matter expertise at many organizations. If 10 different people are asking you for 10 different courses for 10 different reasons at 10 different times, it can be difficult to spot opportunities for strategic consolidation. In chapter 11, we discuss how a holistic, consolidated approach to an organization's compliance library can help to resolve this issue. In the meantime, seize any opportunities you can find to eliminate redundancies between courses and organize similar content around real-world problems.

Tip 5: Give Learners Rich Resources and the Freedom to Fail

The key to problem-based learning is the freedom to approach the problem and seek solutions in one's own way. Whether you are creating an in-person experience or an online tutorial, the more freedom of choice you can offer within the flow of the experience, the better.

Simple enabling devices include the use of self-guided resources, like a binder of relevant policies or a link to an information-rich website, instead of forced resources like lectures or a series of timed slides. If the problems are structured correctly, the learners will need to access all the required content to reach a sufficient solution, so you need not dictate any structure beyond that. If they already know a piece of information, why waste their time in learning it again? If they don't, they will look it up in the provided resources and immediately integrate the new knowledge into its associated context. As an added benefit, they have a chance to practice finding relevant information from a range of resources, which is among the most critical skills for success in any modern profession.

For more complex problems, you may also need to provide additional scaffolding and support to ensure that learners model the appropriate problem-solving strategies. The freedom of minimal guidance approaches can inspire skilled learners and help them achieve more lasting learning outcomes, but results can be diminished if the problem is too challenging or the audience lacks the basic understanding needed for success. As Kirchner, Sweller, and Clark (2006) summarize in their literature review of minimally guided learning techniques such as PBL, "lower aptitude students who choose or were assigned to unguided, weaker instructional treatments receive significantly lower scores on post-tests than on pre-test measures." In other words, freedom and a lack of structure can diminish knowledge if you aren't careful.

Luckily, the research also shows that effective scaffolding of positive strategies can reverse this impact and generate desirable outcomes for any audience. The trick is to provide as much freedom as possible, while also building the structure needed to support less savvy learners and create a consistent learning experience for all. Examples of scaffolding include the use of worksheets or templates that prompt learners to reason through problems in productive ways, or automated alerts in online tutorials that tell learners when they've made a bad decision and provide suggestions when they are stuck in a loop.

However, scaffolding should not reach the level of handholding, and we should not be afraid to let our learners fail, at least temporarily. Real-world problems are challenging for a reason, and providing easy answers only serves to lessen the interest and impact of the learning. Instead, you should be willing to create courses where your learners may occasionally feel lost or confused, as long as the resources and structure are there when needed to help them reach the right conclusion. It is in this moment of genuine need, and only this moment, that genuine learning occurs.

Don't Be Afraid of a Good Problem

In an effort to reinforce policies and avoid legal gray areas, many organizations have gone out of their way to choose simplified nonproblems as the focus of their compliance campaigns. By relying on obvious scenarios, bland exercises, and safe case studies, we've shown our learners again and again that there is nothing to see here. Instead, for the sake of legal compliance, we'll spend a few hours a year pretending to fix something that no one really believes was ever broken in the first place.

The result is lowest-common denominator training, full of thought-provoking lessons like don't steal, don't beat up your co-workers, and don't sexually harass your colleagues. This lack of real and relevant problems may have robbed compliance training of any potential utility in the past, but there's no reason to believe that lack of relevancy is a necessary condition.

In fact, most compliance subjects are rife with genuinely difficult problems waiting to be solved, which is why the training is mandated in the first place. We wouldn't be asked to create training for these subjects by a government agency or regulatory body if someone wasn't already making bad decisions in meaningful situations.

To create an engaging, effective learning experience, we need to identify these genuine dilemmas and present them to our audience honestly, in a way that makes them see the problem for themselves and embrace their stake in finding a solution. The case studies in appendix 4 provide some useful examples, but finding the right problem at your organization may be easier than you think. Problems, unfortunately, are everywhere.

Once we've inspired our learners' natural desire to learn and improve, all we have to do is provide the tools and resources they'll need to reach the right outcomes and get out of their way. The awesome power of their intrinsic motivation will take it from there, preparing them to act as empowered, ethical leaders who can advance the organization's mission and reduce risk in their daily lives. If we quit thinking of compliance in terms of laws and mandates, and start thinking in terms of problems and solutions, our learners will follow—and so will the results.

Chapter 10

Branding, Measurement, and Other Ways to Make or Break Your Compliance Program

In the 1980s, Texas had a litter problem. Highways were strewn with trash, garbage cans were ignored, and the Texas Department of Transportation (TxDOT) was spending $20 million a year to clean it all up.

The state tried to fight the trash problem with laws, warning signs, brochures, and marketing ploys, but for years nothing worked. They simply hadn't found the right message.

Then, in 1985, TxDOT asked a marketing firm how they would combat the problem. The clever firm conceived a broad campaign around a single, simple phrase: "Don't Mess With Texas." The words soon became a sort of unofficial state slogan—and one of the most successful advertising taglines of all time.

Wisely, the first campaign bumper stickers and signs didn't mention litter, trash, or any Texas laws. They just featured those four strong words on a simple background, allowing the phrase to linger in the public imagination and build its own connotations. The words weren't publicly associated with litter until nearly a year later, when the campaign officially launched with a TV ad during the Cotton Bowl featuring blues guitarist and beloved Texan Stevie Ray Vaughan.

The marketers knew that using words like litter and law would have the immediate effect of tuning out those who most needed to hear their message. They looked at their main offending demographic—young men—and knew that their anti-litter message couldn't sound like political correctness or nagging if it was to be effective. It needed to sound like a young Texan talking to his friend, giving it to him straight, as they say. The slogan allowed them to speak the real language of their audience, instead of expecting their audience to decipher the distant language of compliance.

The ad designers integrated the tone of the slogan into the look and feel of the campaign collateral, with trash cans and signs sporting a bold font and bright colors, often including U.S. or Texas flags. They scored further subconscious trust by selecting strong Texas heroes as their spokesmen, and incorporating confident, almost brash swagger in their radio and television ads.

"We thought the way to get it into the public's consciousness quickest was to let Texans own it," said Tom McClure, one of the slogan's creators, in a 2017 interview for *Smithsonian* magazine. "It had that Texas bravado to it, and they adopted 'Don't mess with Texas' as their own battle cry."

The results of the campaign present a compelling case for the possibility of real behavior change. Roadside observations revealed a 29 percent reduction in litter within a year, and a 54 percent reduction the year after that. By 1990, following five sustained years of not messing with Texas, litter rates were down 72 percent from their 1986 high. That's the power of the right words, delivered the right way.

This story of trash in Texas is relevant to our compliance training mission for two important reasons. First, it illustrates the importance of measurement, which we'll discuss near the end of this chapter. If TxDOT hadn't set out to objectively track highway litter rates, it wouldn't have known the state had a problem to solve. The department would have simply kept repeating the same communications techniques forever, scattering its message to the wind and hoping it would eventually stick. Unfortunately, this is not far removed from the approach many compliance training programs currently use. If we're serious about changing behavior, we need to be serious about measurement.

Second, if you expect your measurements to reveal successful change, you need to be sure you're delivering the right message, in the right way. Words, tone, and connotation are extremely powerful tools, and the way you package and present your course can have a massive impact on your outcomes. A great hour-long tutorial that's full of critically important content will amount to little change if its title or description loses your audience's interest before they even begin. Conversely—as Stevie Ray Vaughan has shown us—the right words can change everything.

Success and failure are so often determined by the whims of your brand. How your audience feels about your program is even more important to its results than the information it contains, the habits it seeks to instill, or the problems it hopes to solve. If participants don't believe that your content will offer some benefit to them, it won't.

So, before we conclude with a discussion of measurement, let's explore what it means to craft a compliance brand that speaks the language of your learners, and makes your great content more likely to be heard.

Building a Better Brand for Compliance

Imagine you're an overtaxed employee in a busy corporation. You have project deadlines looming, ambitious metrics to hit, and a range of people in your personal and professional life who are depending on your constant support. Stop me if any of this sounds familiar.

Now, imagine that you receive the following email:

To:	All Employees
From:	Senior AVP's Office of Fraud, Waste, and Abuse
Subject:	**Mandatory Annual Compliance Training**
Message:	Dear Bob,

The annual compliance window this year will run from April 1 to April 30. All current employees are required to complete the program, which includes four one-hour long tutorials, to meet our annual compliance training and reporting requirements.

Click here to launch the program, and be sure to complete all four tutorials by April 30 to avoid potential disciplinary action.

Thank you,
Senior Management

As a busy employee, how are you feeling now? If you're thinking, "I have to remember to click through these four stupid tutorials when I have a minute," you could be forgiven. There's nothing in the email to suggest you should do anything more.

When you do click the link to launch the tutorials and avoid disciplinary action—you're a responsible person, after all—imagine you open the first tutorial to a page of learning objectives that promise little more than mere compliance with the required policies and laws, followed by a slew of content-heavy slides that sound an awful lot like they were written by a lawyer. What do you do? If you answer, "pay as little attention as possible and finish as quickly as possible," congratulations! You are now attuned with the mind of the average learner.

Unfortunately, the above scenario is still the norm at many organizations. But it doesn't have to be. If you've been implementing the tips you discovered in this book, you've already done the hard work to make your compliance courses more meaningful and engaging. You've tailored relevant content to meet the real needs of each audience, instead of creating one-size-fits-all courses that are bound to feel irrelevant to some, if not all, of your learners. You've used the first page of the analysis form to cut everything that isn't expressly required, and you've used the second page to identify real, relevant problems your learning program can actually help solve. You've built meaningful behavioral solutions for those problems that alter your learners' context, modify their problematic habits, and spark their own intrinsic motivation to make the world a better place.

You've already bridged the gap between compliance and learning, crafting a sophisticated program that can change behavior and reduce risk, instead of just mitigating risk and checking boxes. But if you don't make it clear to your learners that this year's program is different—that it actually deserves their attention—all your hard work will be for naught.

Leaving the Old Brand

Past is perception. In the compliance training world, we've spent years squandering our learner's time and eroding their trust. If we want to win back their full attention, we need to use every technique we can in the marketing, packaging, and implementation of our programs to push the reset button on their expectations. We have to clearly signal to our learners that this time is different. We must build a new brand for a new kind of compliance.

Luckily, if old compliance training did nothing else, it did a remarkable job of establishing a very clear brand for us to break from. Traditional compliance training is a thing our learners know all too well—it comes with its own distinct set of cues that tell your learners how little to expect from the experience. If we want to shift expectations, we have to avoid those cues.

For example, never start your course with definitions. They offer little value in any practical setting, and have no place in your course overview, your objectives, or just about anywhere else. All they do is signify to your learners that this is another compliance course that's more interested in definitions than it is in solving real problems. Instead, start with a relevant story that makes the need for your program clear to the learner, and only use definitions to fill in gaps or satisfy specific mandates when needed. Even if a definition is mandated, it shouldn't drive the design or development of your course or hinder its learner-centered look and feel.

By deliberately distancing your compliance program from the old compliance brand—as shown in Exhibit 10-1—you can give your new and improved training the fresh start it deserves.

Exhibit 10-1. Rebranding Your Compliance Training

Old Compliance	New Compliance
Don't name your course after the policy or law to which it is complying: • FERQ Annual Compliance Tutorial 2019 • SDS and PPE Required Lab Training	Name your course in a way that underscores its value to your learners: • Protecting the Power Grid • A Scientist's Guide to Lab Safety
Don't write your objectives with knowledge verbs: • Define, recall, understand, explain	Write your objectives with behavior change verbs: • Leverage, use, avoid, start, stop

Exhibit 10-1. Rebranding Your Compliance Training (cont.)

Old Compliance	New Compliance
Don't assess on definitions, policy details, and other forms of recall: • Which of the following statements best defines the role of a required reporter?	Assess on simulations, scenarios, and real world applications: • Imagine you're a required reporter and a student comes to you for advice about something that happened last weekend. He looks shaken. What should you do?
Don't focus your communication on extrinsic motivation: • You are required to complete this program within 30 days. Failure to comply may result in disciplinary action.	Focus your communication on intrinsic motivation: • This tutorial can help you become a force for positive change within our organization. Please review the tutorial within the next 30 days to learn how you protect yourself, your peers, and your customers.
Don't emphasize arbitrary punishments for failing to comply with the training mandate: • Our records show that you have not yet completed your required training. If you do not complete the program within the next 30 days, you will not be eligible for merit increases during this year's performance review cycle.	Emphasize the real risks of misconduct and the lost value of missed learning: • Our records show that you have not yet completed your required training. Without the benefit of this content, you may be exposing yourself and the organization to serious risks. Please complete the program as soon as possible to begin leveraging critically important skills that may make a significant difference in your professional well-being.
Don't strike a righteous, distant, or overtly legal tone: • All employees are required to take basic safety training within their first 30 days of employment. Please pay careful attention to the tutorial and call your local safety officer if you don't think you'll be able to comply with any of the policies noted therein. You must score at least 80 percent on the final quiz to receive credit for completion.	Write your course and its surrounding communications in your learners' tone: • Here at ACME company, we believe in safety. We expect you to prioritize safety in your daily work, and we know you expect the same of us. To help, we've created a brief tutorial that covers the most important safety practices for your daily work. Take a look, and let your local safety officer know if you have any feedback, concerns, or questions.

Not Just Because We Said So

Too often, compliance teams become wed to the programs they create as if they were hewn in stone. When learners ask why they must comply, or why the learning applies to them, such teams too often reply, essentially, "Because we said so."

This is not only a dangerous reliance on extrinsic motivation. The response undermines your entire effort to build compliance training that matters, by reinforcing the concept that we are only complying for the sake of complying.

If a manager or an employee calls you to complain about training that they don't think applies to them, listen. If possible, allow managers to craft alternative learning plans for their employees that better suit their environment and needs. Such flexibility may be the only way to ensure relevancy for all.

If such flexibility isn't possible in your organization, thank the learner for the feedback and use it to make future courses more relevant.

Don't Forget the Problems You Set Out to Solve

The Compliance Training Analysis Form (appendix 1) helped you identify where the real learning needs exist within your compliance subject. The best way to differentiate your program and win back the trust of your learners is to make sure that those needs are clear and present in everything they see in your program—before, during, and after the training itself. Most importantly, make sure they see results.

It's not enough to create content that's shorter and tighter, or more interesting and engaging to your audience. To achieve your full mandate, you have to be able to show that your training is actually solving the problems you set out to address. If you can't measure your results, all your efforts at reshaping compliance training will amount to little more than window dressing.

When you filled out the Compliance Training Analysis Form, you also outlined the measurements that could demonstrate whether the objectives you chose to highlight were achieved. Once you reach the end of the project, you must follow through on those measurements.

That may seem obvious and simple, but the evaluation step is often skipped on compliance training projects, much to the detriment of our profession. Don't make that mistake. If you don't measure your results, you'll:

- Miss out on convincing evidence that could help win more resources to further improve your L&D offerings, and earn more trust from future SMEs.

- Fail to demonstrate your full commitment to the learners, sending the subconscious message that you don't really care about the training in any meaningful way beyond mere completion (in most corporate settings, any initiative that is worth taking seriously is also worth measuring).

- Never know which learning initiatives succeed or fail, which delivery methods work best for your audience, or which problems you still need to solve. Without post-learning measurement, any genuine improvement in the quality or influence of your training becomes impossible.

Luckily, the value of evaluation and measurement has long been known within the industry, and L&D literature is full of great resources that can help improve your measurement methods and your ability to interpret the hard data into actionable insights. The next generation of learning management systems promises to take measurement capabilities to new heights, providing untapped pools of user data, as well as machine learning algorithms that can help make sense of that data in new ways. It's a good time to be interested in measurement, and if you haven't already joined the big data boom, it's definitely time to start thinking about it. If you don't find ways to demonstrate the actual effectiveness of your compliance training soon, you may find yourself in an impossible position when that data is eventually demanded.

Compliance Measurement Questions

Incomplete data and competing workload often impede measurement and evaluation, but regardless of your constraints, you can't consider a training project finished until you follow through on your intended measurements. In the compliance training space, that measurement is likely to generate some predictable questions. Let's work through a few.

Do Smile Sheets Matter in Compliance?

Smile sheets—a derisive euphemism for the immediate post-learning surveys that constitute Kirkpatrick's Level 1 evaluation—provide metrics with obvious appeal, but limited usefulness. It is satisfying to know that participants enjoyed a session, but that enjoyment does not necessarily correlate with lasting learning transfer or behavior change. Self-assessments from participants about how much they learned, or how much they would recommend the learning experience to a peer, have proven only partially reliable in predicting the kinds of learning outcomes we really want to achieve. Smiles, unfortunately, don't always equal learning.

However, in the world of compliance training, smile sheets can offer real value as a branding tool. If you've never followed up with your audience after an annual compliance campaign to ask about their experience, doing so now may send a clear signal that you are approaching the initiative in a new light. It also shows participants that you're putting the focus back on them, where it belongs. If you can use Level 1 data to further improve your learners' experience in the future, that data can become part of your successful compliance story.

If you also include open-ended questions in the post-training survey—"What did you find most surprising?" or "What would you like to learn next?" or "What challenges do you anticipate when applying this content in the workplace?"—you may also generate useful insights to help jumpstart the analysis phase of next year's project.

How Do I Measure Something Subjective, Like Harassment?

It is more difficult to measure some forms of misconduct than others, and harder still to objectively quantify the data. But just because it's difficult, doesn't mean it's impossible. Nor does it mean that it isn't worth trying.

Begin with a thorough inventory of any related metrics that are already being tracked at your organization, and try to prioritize data sources that are the most robust, long-lasting, and relevant to your subject. For example, if your organization already has a reporting system for safety incidents in the workplace, see how granular the system allows you to get with that data. If you can easily isolate just the incidents involving forklifts, then you have an easy, ready-made metric to measure the effectiveness of any new forklift training program.

For sexual harassment, on the other hand, you may need to rely on many sources of data to see a full picture. You may want to compare the results of climate surveys and exit interviews, pending legal claims and formal complaints, anonymous hotline reports, turnover disparities between women and men, and so on. You may also be able to generate data of your own. For example, some learning management systems allow you to send targeted pulse surveys that ask large portions of your audience about their specific experiences at the organization. If the sample is sufficiently large and random, and the questions are well written, any shifts in the aggregate responses before and after training could be correlated to your program's effectiveness.

What's most important—as we've already stressed—is that you know what measurements you're hoping to affect before you even begin building your course. Behavior change is notoriously difficult. To have any hope of success, we must know exactly what needle we want to move, and exactly what direction we want it to go.

Should Reports of Misconduct Go Up or Down?

For many compliance-training subjects, reports to the organization's ethics hotline or other reporting channels are the only objective metrics available for measurement. If you consider tying your training program's effectiveness to these metrics, your stakeholders are likely to ask the question: Should good training cause these reports to go up by raising awareness, or down by preventing misconduct?

The answer is that good training could achieve either of these results, but obviously not both. The trick is to know which result your organization needs now, and then to design and implement your training with a single-minded focus on achieving that specific outcome.

If you work in a large organization that didn't have any sexual harassment reports last year, that may mean one of two things: either your organization is somehow impervious to the gender-based and sexual misconduct that plague the rest of our society, or people aren't reporting misconduct when it occurs. You may wish to review climate surveys or other anecdotal evidence to be sure, but chances are it's the latter. If so, focus your training on drawing attention to the issue, driving home the reporting mechanisms, and removing any residual fears of retaliation or inaction. If the training is sufficiently well designed and delivered, you can safely expect your number of reported incidents to go up as a result, and that is a good outcome. If harassment is occurring at your organization—and it probably is—it's better for it to be reported than not. Such reporting helps to protect the most vulnerable, remove the most dangerous, and prepare your organization for more effective forms of prevention in the future.

If the reporting culture is already strong at your organization, and the number of sexual harassment reports have been steady over several years, you can target a reduction of reports by focusing your training more on the root causes of harassment. If you can design a course that successfully raises empathy or the ability of bystanders to intervene in the moment of need, you could expect to see the total number of reports decline within the following year.

The measure of success can look very different at different organizations depending on their current climate, their learners, and their needs. What's most important is to determine what success looks like for your training before you start. Otherwise, you'll never know if the results you achieve should count as success or failure, and you'll be no closer to achieving any real behavior change.

What If I Don't Get the Results I Expected?

When Thomas Edison was asked how he persevered through so many failed trials en route to inventing the light bulb, he was apparently somewhat confused by the question. "I didn't fail," he replied simply. "I figured out 10,000 ways not to build a light bulb."

Failure, if viewed correctly, is nothing more than another step on the path to success. If you measure the effectiveness of your training programs and discover that they aren't really making a difference, that's great news! You just eliminated one solution that won't work, and took an important step closer to the solution that will.

A Virtuous Cycle

Let's think back to the dramatic reduction in Texas litter that we discussed at the beginning of this chapter. That 72 percent reduction in just four years—a truly transformative result—revealed the immense impact that proactive training and communication can have when we take it seriously. We only have to start with real behavior change as our goal, and keep our eyes forever locked on that target.

While "Don't mess with Texas" didn't achieve that 72 percent reduction on its own, the initial campaign and its accompanying measurements had a hand in every piece of litter kept off the streets since. The campaign succeeded in such dramatic fashion because it succeeded in shifting the momentum of human behavior.

The simplicity of the initial campaign produced an immediate, if modest, return; and the measurement of that return offered rich opportunities for further improvement. With a strong foundation now in place, Texas could investigate and invest in specific roads where high litter rates remained unchanged, broaden their campaign to reach new audiences, and focus the power of their message on more productive habits. The foundation of that successful campaign prompted a virtuous cycle, the ultimate results of which was a world far removed—and far cleaner—from the world in which it began.

Your new and improved compliance training can spark similar cycles within your organization, with equally far-reaching results. By shifting context, honing habits, and harnessing your learners' motivation—by focusing every minute of your training on real problems and real solutions—you will generate measurable behavior change. Those changes may be modest at first—a few extra visits to an ethics resource page per month, a few extra harassment reports per year, a few points of improvement on your next climate survey—but change begets change, and small changes today can loom large over time.

With each new problem your training solves, you reduce a little more risk, earn a little more trust from your learners, and raise the standard of behavior at your organization a little higher. The higher that bar rises, the higher still your learners will come to expect. The result is a self-sustaining culture of ethics and compliance that is resilient to small changes in climate or leadership—a culture that knows its values, and serves those values well.

The strengths of such a culture would easily transcend the training tips and tricks we've discussed within this book. But if you hope to one day enjoy its benefits, behavioral compliance training is the only way to start.

PART 3:
THE FUTURE

Chapter 11
Consolidated Compliance

Due to the rising scope of compliance subjects and the rising expectations of organizational accountability documented in part 1, the compliance training industry finds itself in need of total reconstruction. Beyond the surgical improvements outlined in part 2, which can immediately yield tangible results, our most vexing problems likely can't be solved without a total tear down and rebuild of the way we think about compliance subjects and envision compliance training.

The traditional method of establishing exhaustive policies and heavy-handed training programs is proving less popular, less sustainable, and less effective in managing risk than modern audiences, executives, and regulators are willing to tolerate. The new organization wants less cynical dogma and more strategic support from its leadership and compliance team. Wise compliance experts are eager to rise to that challenge, as we've seen in earlier chapters, and learning professionals are ready to help them reach the new bar.

But to best serve our learners and maximize our impact on misconduct, we need to reimagine the full compliance program with learning and learners at its center. Instead of finding opportunities for great training within the artificial constraints of laws and policies—which we achieved in earlier chapters by completing the Compliance Training Analysis Form—we need to start putting our faith in the power of learning and individual decision making, with policies and laws left only as a safety net.

In other words, we need to start thinking of ethics and compliance learning as an end in and of itself, rather than a piecemeal smattering of subjects thrown together to comply with myriad laws and regulations, with as much focus on the learner as we can muster along the way.

To reach that target, we must convince our organizations to give us the time and resources required to assure that our compliance learning efforts are designed strategically to optimize two critically important criteria:

- We are achieving the maximum possible impact with our compliance learning, reducing real risk and advancing our organization's mission.

- We are meeting our minimum legal training requirements as efficiently as possible.

Given the huge number of compliance subjects already filling our collective learning libraries, and the droves likely to come in the years ahead, a program offering anything less than these two criteria would be performing a massive disservice to our learners and our organizations. To put it frankly, anything less than a program that hits both these targets is wasting valuable time and resources.

To ensure that our compliance programs are never a waste of time, we need to stop thinking of compliance training as a series of distinct and unconnected battles, each waged by a different SME in hopes of staving off a different law or regulatory requirement. Instead, compliance training must be approached as a sophisticated war for ethical behavior, with new battles fought only when strategically called for. We need to make our professional learning departments and talent development offices the headquarters for this new campaign, and we all need to take our marching orders from one new general: the learner.

Obstacles to Learner-Centered, Transformative Compliance

There are three practical reasons why bad compliance training has flourished for so long. If we want to reach our full potential, we'll need to go beyond the lessons of the previous chapters and adopt a holistic learning plan that removes these obstacles once and for all.

Traditional Compliance Training Programs Are Siloed

If you're lucky, your organization might have a chief ethics officer or similarly titled executive who is tasked with overseeing strategy for all compliance and ethics subjects at your organization. If you are lucky, this individual will have prioritized training and behavior change as the focus of their collective programs. However, even then, you will likely discover that this commitment to good learning is locked away within the carefully delineated confines of each new compliance subject. In other words, instead of thinking holistically about sexual harassment, many organizations find themselves introducing new courses and programs for every new sexual harassment policy or law that comes along.

Each new law or initiative may effect a slightly different area of the organization, which may lead to the appointment of a new SME and the crafting of new internal policies, programs, and training. These new initiatives probably overlap—slightly or extremely—with existing policies, programs, and responsibilities. This phenomenon is responsible for the compliance bloat we discussed in chapter 1, and it's one of the biggest obstacles we face if we hope to create compliance training that's truly focused on the needs and constraints of our learners.

For example, in my organization, Title IX, the Campus SAVE Act, the Clery Reporting Act, an internal Georgia Tech policy, and a University System of Georgia policy all attempt to eliminate sexual harassment, discrimination, and violence in the campus community. There is great deal of overlap between these laws and policies, and yet my learning team has been asked to develop four different tutorials, addressing essentially the same subjects, by four different departments in just the last two years. If we'd said yes and created four new tutorials for our audience to sit through, the consequences would be dire. At best, we'd be wasting our learners' time and losing their faith in our learning strategy. At worst, we'd be cheapening the message of our tutorials and making the job of improving gender equality and safety on college campuses even more difficult.

This is clearly an important cause that's worth addressing on multiple occasions in multiple ways. However, recurring treatments of the subject must be careful and strategic, focusing on contextual support, timely updates, and behavioral reinforcement. Repetition prompted only by siloes and a lack of centralized strategy is as dangerous as saying nothing at all.

Traditional Compliance Training Programs Are One-Size-Fits-All

Have you ever been asked to practice lifting boxes at work in an apparent nod to warehouse safety, despite the fact that you don't work in a warehouse and rarely lift more than a piece of paper? Have you ever been forced to sit through a tutorial on banking safeguards or the protections in your industry against defrauding customers, despite the fact that you work in HR and have no idea how you would go about defrauding a customer if you wanted to?

Even if your answer to the above questions is no, the odds are high that you have completed at least one tutorial or training course in your career that you've struggled to apply to your daily reality. Instructional designers could quickly tell you why this is a serious problem—adult learners must be motivated to learn, after all, and relevant content is the first and last tool we have for winning that motivation—and yet we continue to subject too many learners to courses that have nothing to do with them or their needs.

One explanation for this obstacle is the traditional risk management paradigm that we discussed in chapter 3. If your primary goal is to mitigate the impact of risk by arguing in court that some bad actor had been trained not to act badly, then you have a clear incentive to train everyone on everything. Sure, there's a 99 percent chance that your poor, busy HR professional will never lay their eyes on a customer's bank account, but you might as well subject them to the training anyway. You've already built it, after all, so you might as well mitigate as much risk with it as possible. Call it erring on the side of caution.

Unfortunately, the side of caution in this case has some serious thorns. When compliance subjects were few and learning systems were limited in their functionality, blanket compliance programs made the most sense. It was easier and cheaper to make everyone in the organization complete the same series of required courses during the same universal compliance windows, instead of building complex programs and oversight schemes tailored to each individual user. Without the right tools, an individually tailored approach at a medium to large organization would require far too many administrative resources to maintain.

However, the growing scope of modern compliance threatens to consume an untenable portion of our employees' time, and we must start making strategic decisions about how that limited time should be allotted. Luckily, that need is coinciding with a rise in next-generation learning management systems that excel at targeting specific learning at specific learners, as we'll discuss in the final chapter.

Traditional Compliance Training Programs Are an Afterthought

Consider the life cycle of the average compliance training subject. Where does it begin?

Typically, it starts with a new a law or regulation, or new guidance on an old law. Sometimes, it begins when previously ignored subjects win new interest from your leadership, typically when current events bring a forgotten risk front of mind. In any of these cases, the request for a new project rarely goes straight to the L&D team. Instead, that request almost always goes to the SMEs, who immediately set about doing what they do best. They follow the risk management playbook, crafting policies, implementing oversight, establishing reporting channels, and enacting each pillar of the traditional compliance program, eventually including the last pillar: training.

This is the point where part 2 of this book picks up, with the instructional designer heeding the call for a new course and springing into an opportunistic analysis phase, hoping to uncover some genuine needs that will make this newly required subject interesting and useful to their learners. Unfortunately, by the time the learning and development team enters the scene, it may be too late to do any real good. The SME has already spent weeks establishing what they think they want, and they have no shortage of policy points and program elements to cram into a new tutorial. They may even bring a finished PowerPoint to your very first meeting, asking only that you put it online. Such SMEs are prepared to fill page 1 of your Compliance Training Analysis Form to the brim, leaving little time or energy for the more important second page, where the real behavioral magic can happen.

Often, by the time the learning team gets involved, there's no time left for analysis, design, or even identifying an audience. There's only time to take the SME's content and give it a quick sprucing up. Then, once you put it out into the world, it will sit in your learning library alongside all the other compliance tutorials that you've rushed to finish for other demanding SMEs. You might try to find time to go back, start from scratch, and make it better someday, but unless we can find a way to break this cycle, that day will never come.

* * *

Any learning professional could see why these obstacles have been so damaging to our compliance training efforts. If we're forced to create a library of redundant tutorials, we are going to waste our learners' finite attention span and dilute the effectiveness of our message. If we're forced to create tutorials that can apply equally to everyone, we will end up with learning that doesn't apply very well to anyone. And if we're an afterthought in the compliance process, we cannot conduct the analysis and design required to uncover our learners' real needs or create effective behavioral solutions. We can't put the best practices of the previous chapters into full effect until L&D gets more say in the overall compliance process.

A New Foundation for Compliance

The call for a brand-new approach to compliance training should by now be clear. As learning professionals, we need a more effective and efficient method for ingesting, organizing, and satisfying compliance training mandates, and a new way of gauging whether those efforts are successful. If compliance training projects used to begin and end with the opinion of the SME, we need the next generation of compliance programs to begin and end with the needs of the learner.

By flipping the three obstacles that have traditionally held us back, we can see an outline of an ideal approach to compliance training, and a path to strategically plan our compliance training efforts across an entire organization:

- **New compliance learning plans are consolidated.** Before we can make compliance learning effective, we have to make it efficient. That requires a zero-tolerance approach to redundancy, and the strategic consolidation of similar subjects into learning programs organized around similar behavioral needs.

- **New compliance learning plans target impactful content to relevant audiences.** We must approach each compliance training project as a collection of relevant learning objectives, matching the right skills and knowledge to the right audiences to engage, inspire, and promote real behavior change.

- **New compliance learning plans start with learning.** To achieve this new combination of efficiency and efficacy, learning professionals need to take a driving role in the planning and evaluation of all compliance training across the entire organization. If we continue to be an afterthought, added near the final implementation of every new compliance program that comes along, we will never be able to break free of the compliance training obstacles we've discussed and deliver our full potential value to the organization.

By buying into these three new pillars and using them to guide the next generation of organizational compliance programs, we can take our training and our broader risk-prevention strategies to new heights. But we need a strategy for that shift, especially in the short term, and that strategy must usher in all this added value without jeopardizing existing benefits or creating any new risks.

This is a complex endeavor with high stakes, many competing priorities, and a broad collection of stakeholders. To navigate this compliance jungle and arrive at the lofty destination we seek, it will help to have a map.

The Eight-Step Road Map to Implementing Your Own Compliance Learning Plan

The traditional obstacles to learner-centered, consolidated compliance existed for a reason, and those obstacles won't disappear without a plan.

This eight-step process can help you strategically advance the quality and impact of your organization's compliance programs, while avoiding potential pitfalls along the way.

Step 1: Form an Organization-Wide Compliance Learning Committee

Who are the best advocates for learning in your organization? Who among those champions also have organizational clout? These are the partners you will need to help chaperone your new compliance training plan into existence.

Winning over every SME may be an impossible task, but winning over a few key stakeholders—like CEOs, vice presidents, head legal counsels, chief ethics officers, or risk management department heads—can be just as effective.

At Georgia Tech, we formed a Compliance Learning Committee of four individuals who had sole authority for reviewing and approving all new content for the annual compliance training campaign. The team included the head of our learning and development department, a lawyer from the Office of Legal Affairs, a long-serving representative from the Office of Internal Audit, and the head ethics officer for one of the most powerful units on campus. These four people had the full faith or their department and the autonomy to make final decisions regarding content. Even more important, they believed in the mission of creating behavioral, learner-centered compliance training.

Build your team, get their buy-in, and don't make the mistake of giving them nothing to do. This group will be critical to your long-term success, so you must keep them engaged and motivated from the start. Luckily, as you will see in step 2, their expertise serves an immediate need.

Step 2: Consolidate Existing Compliance Courses Into Behavioral Categories

Find a list of every compliance SME at your organization and their compliance training subjects. If the list doesn't already exist, enlist your compliance learning committee's help to create one.

If you're looking at a full list for a large organization, there's a good chance you will see more than 50 subjects. At Georgia Tech, our initial list included 74 training subjects, and several new subjects have been added in the years since. To organize such a list, a deliberate structure is essential. To maximize your behavioral impact, that structure should be built not from your understanding of the legal landscape, but from an understanding of your learners and their behavior.

As a starting point, you may wish to use the seven compliance categories outlined in chapter 1: consumer protections, employee protections, civility and diversity, responsible stewardship, fraud and corruption, data privacy and cyber security, and ethics and integrity. As you work through the list, you may find that variations of those categories are more appropriate for your audience. What's most important is that you commit to a basic structure you can use to start consolidating disparate compliance training offerings into a single, overarching plan.

Ultimately, we must find strategic ways to consolidate requirements and needs, and that starts with a carefully designed structure of compliance training categories. Once you have that structure, and the full list of subjects and SMEs that exist within each category, you can proceed to step 3.

Why Consolidate?

Consolidating subjects around learners' needs allows you to create comprehensive programs that offer the maximum impact while wasting as little time as possible. But even if your organization isn't ready to prioritize the learner above all, the call for consolidation may still be clear.

Learning and development teams are continuously asked to create a new course for every new law or mandate that arises, and then asked to update that massive library of courses whenever any of the laws change. That's not a tenable scope for success, and it's only going to get more daunting in the years ahead. Even if we had the ability to glue our eyes open and crank out separate courses for every subject that compliance law mandates in the future, our learners would have no time left after training to actually do their jobs.

Step 3: Document Specific Legal Requirements for Each Category

In chapter 5, we introduced the Compliance Training Analysis Form as powerful tool for successfully launching any new compliance training project. This is a key resource in your new consolidated approach, too. At its essence, the form allows you to balance real behavioral needs with concrete mandates to best meet the needs of your learners and your SMEs. It can help dramatically improve the quality and efficiency of your individual courses and tutorials, but it works best when completed for an entire category.

For example, let's take cyber security as a compliance category. Page 1 of the Compliance Training Analysis Form asks you to consider the laws or policies within that category that include a specified training requirement for your industry. Then it asks what the specific requirements are. If the laws or policies only require some version of the generic, "all employees must receive annual training," then you have total leeway to design a plan in this category based only on your learners' needs. On the other hand, if any laws include specific content or hour requirements for specific audiences, it pays to know that early.

The goal is to replace every cyber security course you currently have with a single, unified training plan for that entire category—a plan that distributes the universal components of each law to your entire audience as efficiently as possible, and targets behavioral content at specific audiences where it can have the most impact, as you will see in steps 4 and 5.

If your SMEs are reluctant to allow this consolidation, lean on your compliance learning committee for support. Ultimately, if your organization is found in violation of a cyber law or regulation, and a judge is tallying your aggravating and mitigating factors to determine a sentence, that judge will only care that training existed, that it met any minimum legal requirements, and that the offenders were exposed to the training prior to offending. If you have an especially progressive judge, they may also care about the pedagogical quality of that training and whether it was intended to prevent the risk instead of just checking a box. But they certainly won't care what the training was called, or whether it was consolidated with training to satisfy other laws that sought to achieve the same ends. Convincing your SMEs of this simple truth—that we can focus our training efforts on reducing risk without jeopardizing our ability to mitigate that risk—is the first step to creating truly relevant learning.

Step 4: Conduct a Risk Assessment in Each Category

Risk assessments are an extremely fruitful exercise. By asking your compliance learning committee to conduct a risk assessment within each category, you underscore the role of training as a serious player in the risk management discussion, win the buy-in of risk-preoccupied SMEs and senior leaders, and add another prong to your potential legal defense. By starting your training plan with a real risk analysis, you allow your organization to argue honestly in court that your learning events were created in direct response to internally identified risks. Such risk assessments were specifically listed as an important mitigating factor in the 2004 amendment to the Federal Sentencing Guidelines.

Most importantly, the risk assessment can serve as the foundation for your entire analysis phase by providing your instructional design team with a list of outcomes that your learning objectives should serve. By aligning your learning with the real risks that your organizational leadership has recognized themselves, you ensure that your final training program will be seen as valuable, and that learning and development begins to be seen as a real business driver.

In step 5, returning our attention to the Compliance Training Analysis Form, the instructional design team will break these risks down into their component behaviors, and then create a menu of solutions to change those behaviors by creating targeted training for targeted audiences.

What Is a Risk Assessment?

Risk assessments have been a mainstay in the business world for decades, and there are a number of free models available online if you'd like a template to guide your approach. Whatever model you choose, be sure your executives include both the severity of potential risks and the likelihood when determining which risks require the most aggressive management plans.

Step 5: Create Behavior-Based Objectives Targeting Relevant Audiences

If we give up on teaching everything to everyone, then questions immediately arise about what exactly we will teach and to whom. Answering those questions effectively requires continuous collaboration and careful thought, and the second page of the Compliance Training Analysis Form can provide much needed structure for those discussions.

Within each category, the form prompts you to consider how specific risks could be reduced by helping specific audiences change specific behaviors. For example, let's return to the category of cyber security. Perhaps your leadership team discovered in step 4 that a high-profile data breach is a risk that demands immediate attention, and you've decided to make reducing that risk the focus of all your cyber security training. How would you go about reducing that risk?

Tips for behavioral analysis and design were provided in part 2 of this book, but it's important to reiterate that the behaviors most relevant to your risk should be the primary focus of your training, and that making a serious impact on the likelihood of the risk will likely require you to target different behaviors for different audiences. In the cyber security example, you may decide to implement a series of courses and other learning solutions that:

- Help all employees learn techniques to avoid being phished or hacked by clicking on the wrong link or responding to the wrong email.
- Help IT professionals understand the categories of data in your organization, and the practical safeguards they should be implementing whenever building new reports, applications, or websites.
- Help customer-facing associates recognize sensitive data they may come in contact with, and techniques for safely destroying or sequestering this data in their standard customer service workflow.

The objectives that will have the most impact for you will depend on your audience, your organization's greatest areas of risk, and the types and scale of training tools available to you. Once you commit to putting behavioral needs ahead of compliance, the best opportunities for real learning are often readily apparent.

Step 6: Check Any Remaining Boxes As Efficiently As Possible

In the first five steps, we've prioritized consolidation of compliance mandates around behavioral needs. For example, instead of having six courses for the six sexual harassment laws that apply to your industry, you can unite the shared principles of all six laws into a single training plan that focuses only on the real behavioral needs that your audience is experiencing regarding gender equality, discrimination, civility, or harassment. But what if some of those laws and mandates have specific training requirements that your behavior-focused courses no longer meet?

To ensure your final training plan retains its full risk-management appeal, step 6 allows SMEs and learning professionals to work backward to ensure the prongs of your unified plan also meet every specific legal requirement stipulated by each applicable law or policy, which you recorded on page 1 of the Compliance Training Analysis Form during step 3.

If you discover that one of the laws requires a specific definition, or the sharing of a specific policy point or reporting channel, then you will need to work that into some or all of your deliverables, depending on the structure of your plan, the mandate, and the audiences for which it is required. The trick is to meet these abstract legal requirements as efficiently as possible. Don't repeat the information any more than necessary to ensure it reaches the required population, and don't allow it to distract from your behavior-focused content any more than it has to.

Self-paced slides in online courses can be a great way to address these kinds of needs. By stopping the main action of your tutorial at a convenient breaking point, you can provide a list of required definitions or policies for your audience to review at their own pace, allowing them to choose when they are ready to continue with the more relevant, behavioral meat of your course.

What About Training Hour Requirements?

Hour requirements are the only exception to the rule of considering compliance mandates after behavior needs. If you know your state requires eight hours of sexual harassment training for every employee each year, it's best to know that up front and design your approach accordingly. You may need to cast a broader net during your behavioral analysis for such courses, because you know you will need at least eight hours of relevant content. While the savvy learning professional would prefer to focus all the audience's attention on two or three of the most pressing objectives, hour requirements may force you to include objectives that would not have otherwise made the cut.

Step 7: Evaluate and Iterate

The Compliance Training Analysis Form includes space to consider what measurements will be used to show whether each behavioral objective has been achieved. That's the beautiful thing about behavior: it can be observed and it leaves tracks.

Once your compliance training plan has been implemented, be sure to follow through by actually conducting these measurements. If behavior has changed in a measurable way, you can use this to justify the added effort of consolidating compliance subjects in other categories in the future. It will also help to further mitigate your risk in the event of a lawsuit by proving the effectiveness of your training.

Even more important, if you discover that behavior has not changed as intended, you can return to the beginning and devise new solutions, repeating the process of trial and error until you find the combination of learning experiences and situational initiatives that actually move the needle.

Step 8: Prioritize Efficiency and Efficacy When Addressing New Mandates

Change is the only constant in life, and that is especially true of compliance. New laws and mandates come into existence every day, and existing laws are constantly being redefined by the latest legal interpretations. As a result, your instructional design team and compliance training committee will be constantly approached by new SMEs requesting new training programs to satisfy the latest iteration of their compliance mandates.

The hard work you have already put into your consolidated compliance training plans will pay dividends during the start of these new projects. To prioritize new work, you must only work with the SME to answer the following three questions:

- Which consolidated category does this new training mandate fit into?
- Does this mandate present new opportunities for relevant behavior change? If so, what are those needs?
- Does this new mandate present specific training requirements beyond those already addressed by our existing training in this category? If so, how can our existing plan be amended as efficiently as possible to meet these new requirements without wasting the learners' time or distracting from our behavioral focus?

If the new mandate only requires you to mention a single new policy, and you already have a self-paced slide outlining policies in an existing tutorial, meeting the new demand may be as easy as adding one more item to a list. On the other hand, if the subject is completely new or was created in response to a previously nonexistent risk, this may be a great opportunity to create a brand-new compliance category and strategy, or to add a new learning experience to an existing category.

With a compliance learning committee and your consolidated compliance learning plans in place, you are in an excellent position to make those decisions in the best interest of your learners and your organization, instead of just throwing another tutorial on the compliance heap.

If You Can't Win Big, Win Small

I've been teaching an ATD Essentials course on compliance training design for the last several years, and there is a point in every class when I start to feel a little guilty.

The course is a lot of fun, and at first we all just enjoy sharing stories of difficult SMEs and commiserating on the challenge of building good training with our limited time, budgets, and organizational clout. Before long, we're brainstorming visions of how great compliance training could be, envisioning best-in-class programs that win back our learners' trust and make the world a genuinely better place. But inevitably, at some point, someone speaks the voice of doubt: "This is obviously right," they usually say, "but it's never going to happen for me."

"My organization has done the same things the same way for so long, they're never going to change," they continue. "They don't even believe in real learning. Why are they going to waste time and money on trying something they don't think will work anyway, when the way they've been managing legal risk has been working for years?"

To those questions, all I can say is . . . you're right. And I've been there.

It's going to be difficult if not impossible to implement a full compliance training plan overnight at many status quo organizations. You need at least one learning champion in a position of real power if you hope to get any traction, and you will likely need more than that if you expect the plan to stick.

The good news is, we don't have to solve this entire problem overnight. While a fully consolidated compliance training program is likely the only long-term solution that can truly balance the needs of our learners and our lawyers, there are steps we could be taking now to move us closer to that ideal. And those little wins could already be making life better for our learners.

For example, when you do find a SME who is passionate about learning, carve out as much time and resources as possible to build a truly outstanding course or program. Consider it a pilot for better compliance training to come, and don't be surprised if other SMEs at your organization start asking for the same treatment for their compliance subjects. It can be hard to explain your intentions to non–learning professionals in a way that allows them to share your excitement, but once your stakeholders see what a good training solution really looks like, they'll want more.

For your more reluctant SMEs, choose your battles and try to make every course as good as possible by drawing strategic lines in the sand where they can return the most value for your learners. Maybe you could convince a SME to cut the most redundant 15 minutes of material from a bloated course, or convince another to focus two separate tutorials on two different audiences, targeting more relevant content than one blanket tutorial ever could. These small adjustments aren't enough to fix all the ills of compliance training on their own, but they help. By standing up for the learner and making small changes where they can have the biggest impact, you can wage a war of attrition that will eventually lead to the same lean, learner-centered, consolidated catalog that this chapter is striving to help you achieve. It may take a little longer to get there, but if the long path is the only path available, you owe it to your learners to start hiking.

Whether you are designing holistic training plans based on consolidated behavioral categories, or revising a single tutorial to meet the training demands of a single SME, the tips and tricks in this book can help you make the final result as engaging and impactful for your learners as possible. You may not be able to implement every tip on every project, but don't be discouraged. If you can't win big, you can at least win small.

And if you can string enough small wins together, you may be surprised to discover that your power in the organization has grown dramatically, that misconduct has plummeted, and that compliance training looks very different than it did when you began. In fact, you may wake up one day to find that compliance training no longer exists at all, at least not in a form any of us would recognize. And what a beautiful day that would be.

Chapter 12
The End of Compliance

If instructional designers and learning professionals can take a more proactive, assertive role in shaping behavioral compliance training—as this book has outlined—our learners will soon enjoy a period of dramatic improvement in the quality and usefulness of their required compliance training. Following that period, if we reach our full potential, compliance training will cease to exist.

It may seem strange to write a book that aims to make itself obsolete, but in a perfect world, that's exactly what it will become. Like a home remedy guide for polio, or a user manual for a steam engine, this book only hopes to be a useful tool for its time and place. If it's useful enough, that time should soon pass.

That is not to say that instructional designers should be looking for a new line of work, or that employee training should take a backseat in the organizations of the future. In fact, exciting new technologies have us poised for a golden age of corporate learning and development, where learning teams can finally demonstrate their return on investment in absolute terms, and win a seat at the table with the organization's most trusted leaders.

No, learning and development will not disappear anytime soon. But compliance training, as we know it, certainly could.

Beyond Compliance

Compliance training has existed for long enough that most of us can no longer imagine a world without it. We may succeed in changing its brand and its usefulness, but it's hard to envision a modern corporation without the most fundamental trademarks of a traditional compliance training program, at least in some form. We still expect compliance to be mandated from time to time. We still expect it to be full of policies and laws. We still expect it to tell us what we can and can't do.

If we wish to create training that is truly learner centered and transformational, we must eventually leave all of those trademarks behind. If we are to progress as a society, as organizations, and as individuals, we need to fully dispel the notion that mere "compliance" was ever enough. Instead, we must return to the business of real learning and development.

In practice, in the organization of the future, compliance training should be replaced by proactive, preventative learning plans that target the specific behaviors necessary to reduce risk at the organization—and nothing more. For example, if an organization enacted four programs—empathy training, embedded ethics and values-based decision-making training, integrated skills training, and predictive prevention—there would be no need for further compliance training. These initiatives would provide the same sense of organizational accountability and legal cover that we have traditionally cobbled together from mandatory compliance tutorials. Even more importantly, they would do a better job of reducing real risk, without any of the added ills that mandatory, inflexible, legally motivated compliance training inevitably creates.

By targeting real needs and only real needs, a new kind of employee training—without compliance—can save our learners' time and earn back their trust. It could also save our organizations from the terrible costs of misconduct better than a thousand compliance tutorials ever could.

Empathy Training

If you could teach your employees a single skill to reduce risk and improve the bottom line, wouldn't that skill be empathy?

Our ability to empathize with one another is a known metric for the success of salespeople, managers, and customer service agents, but its benefits extend well beyond those limited roles. Empathetic leadership can anticipate problems, reduce misconduct, and make our goals a little more likely to be achieved. With empathy at every level of the organization, we can react appropriately to any new dilemma we face. Without empathy, the next bad headline is always just about to print.

We have collectively suffered in the past from a static notion of core virtues like empathy. Empathy is rarely even mentioned in traditional compliance training, suggesting an underlying assumption that it is something you either have or you don't. Promising recent research, however, suggests that empathy is a skill like any other—one that can be developed, sometimes far more easily than we might imagine.

A study by David Kidd and Emanuele Castano (2013), for example, found that empathy could be measurably improved by reading literary fiction. Using simple theory of mind tasks as a rubric—like the ability to identify emotions in pictures of human faces, and the ability to predict the actions of others based on their stated beliefs—the researchers found a measurable spike in participant ability after reading just one short passage of good literary fiction.

A more recent study by Paul Zak at Claremont Graduate University demonstrated similar effects from short, emotive videos. Their video—with relatable characters and high emotional appeal—increased the hormones that promote trust and empathy within its viewers, who subsequently offered larger charitable donations than peers in a control group who did not have their empathy primed.

Virtual reality technologies promise even more empathy in the years ahead. By creating immersive experiences that are increasingly indistinguishable from lived memories, VR offers unprecedented opportunities for emotional intelligence, mindfulness, and empathetic decision making.

Numerous studies have shown spikes in charitable giving following VR encounters that allow participants to experience the need for their donations would help to address. An especially interesting study in 2013 showed that participants who were made to perform a task through simulated colorblindness in a VR lab volunteered twice as much time to improving accessibility for colorblind individuals as those who had only read about and imagined colorblindness. VR allowed those individuals to see the world through someone else's eyes, and the results were dramatic.

Imagine the power of a full VR training series at your organization, allowing every manager to spend a few minutes a month experiencing the world from someone else's perspective. Imagine if these managers could feel the impact of harassment, discrimination, and unsafe practices first-hand, often enough for those simulated experiences to become an ingrained aspect of their worldview. Wouldn't their empathy be likely to rise from those experiences? And with that rise, wouldn't misconduct be likely to fall? Perspective, after all, is a powerful tool.

Embedded Ethics and Values-Based Decision Making

Classical compliance training has done little to develop the decision-making faculties of our learners. If anything, we've created compliance programs that erode decision making by insisting only on rigid adherence to set policies, definitions, and protocols. We've outsourced ethics to our policy libraries, and our culture has suffered as a result.

To transform that culture and take our behavioral progress to new heights, we'll need to quit thinking of our employees as subjects to be governed, and start empowering them to act as ethical leaders. To maintain the highest standards of behavior today, policies alone will never be enough. Instead, ethics has to become a dialogue, and our employees need to take an active role in the conversation. Training based on values, ethical dilemmas, and decision making—instead of policies, rules, and definitions—is the best way to get that conversation started.

At Georgia Tech, we've met this need through the Four Ethical Corners, an ethical decision-making class that offers a four-step framework for reaching sound, defensible decisions in any situation. The framework empowers employees to consider all relevant facts and outcomes before choosing an action that best serves their intention within any existing constraints. Participants are sent back to the office with a two-page decision-making guide and access to an online decision-making app, allowing them to apply the framework consistently to any future dilemmas they face. More importantly, they have a clear understanding that the organization expects them to be far more than rule followers and policy hawks. We need them to be ethical leaders—leaders we can trust to make the right decision in the moment of need without us there to hold their hands.

Integrated Skills Training

By repeatedly pleading with our employees to read policies, follow procedures, and avoid a laundry list of potential misconduct, traditional compliance training has inadvertently suggested to our employees that proper conduct is fragile. We seem to be telling them that doing the right thing is a choice. A choice we are apparently terrified they won't make.

We would never have an annual training program reminding our employees to show up for work, or reminding accountants to double check their math. We would never have widget builders sit through a course that tells them to keep building widgets. We rightly assume, instead, that our employees will simply do their jobs. And yet, for some reason, we think they must be told to be ethical.

Instead of compliance training being something separate from our core job responsibilities—and by implication, optional—we must remove the artificial line between the two. We must dispel the false distinctions between doing a job, and doing the job right. In short, we must eliminate the imagined silo around ethics and compliance.

If you're training your web designers on how to use internal tools to build company websites, the process should naturally include steps that make those websites accessible, secure, and respectful of your customers' private data. You are not separating those steps from the rest of the process, or tacking them on at the end to appease some arbitrary set of compliance laws. They are simply part of what it means to build a website. To skip those steps would be to fail at the most fundamental requirements of the position, resulting in a product that fails to meet the minimum viable standards of completion. It's the same as not showing up for work at all, or an accountant posting transactions that simply don't add up. It's not above or apart from the job; it is the job.

Manager onboarding should include hiring, progressive discipline, and performance management training that incorporates ethical decision making, diversity and inclusion, safety, privacy, and more. Not as compliance add-ons or nice-to-haves, but as fundamental components of what it means to be manager. Learning to drive a forklift should naturally entail learning to drive it safely. Excellent customer service agents should be trained, measured, and rewarded not just on their ability to meet a customer's needs quickly, but also the ability to preserve the customer's privacy in the process. In this promising future, skills that help protect customer privacy wouldn't be presented as another box to check. Instead, they would become an inextricable part of what we mean when we say customer service.

Creating training to meet the many needs traditionally satisfied by compliance training could be a relatively easy task for savvy instructional designers, who excel at mapping performance goals to the necessary skills and knowledge. Once we know what it takes to do a job right, we can build training plans and support tools that our learners actually want and need, and make more measurable changes to behavior as a result.

If your organization is serious about reducing misconduct, the right way must become the only way, and good skills training must be there to help.

Predictive Prevention

"We are rapidly nearing the point where we can confidently tell managers and senior leaders exactly what they stand to gain from training," says JD Dillon, speaker, writer, and chief learning architect for Axonify. "If your employees complete this two-hour learning series, they'll be 20 percent more productive for the next three months. That's not just our opinion, or some abstract application of adult learning theory. It's the data, and it doesn't lie. That's a powerful position for learning and development to occupy."

Thanks to microlearning systems like Axonify, universal data specifications like xAPI, and an ever-growing weave of HR and technical system integrations, many organizations now enjoy a fuller picture of our learners than ever before. Modern learning management systems provide a sharper view of what's happening within learning experiences, and integrated performance management systems make it easier to correlate that learning to real results. Machine learning promises to help us make sense of all that data, revealing trends that may ultimately allow us to predict and influence the future.

It may sound like science fiction, but it's already a reality in many industries. The Atlanta Fire Department uses historic data and predictive analytics to target their fire inspections at properties deemed most at risk by their algorithms, and have enjoyed an observable decline in total fires as a result. Police departments from Pittsburg to Los Angeles employ a similar approach, dispatching their units in any given night to the areas where the data says a crime is most likely to occur. Instead of randomly assigning patrols—or plotting maps based on experience, bias, or conventional wisdom—the data guide their hand. The approach raises some serious ethical questions of its own—including issues of profiling and probable cause—but responsible big data still provides an unprecedented opportunity to align resources with mission. As we generate more data regarding learning and the most frequent forms of misconduct at our organization, the same tools could help us allocate employee training hours with much greater efficiency.

Simple reminder training—not unlike the basic compliance tutorials of years past—can become a far more powerful tool if delivered to the right audience, in the right moment. For example, what if you discovered that the majority of your organization's procurement violations are attributable to a small percentage of your population, always during the same period at the end of each fiscal year? If you could target those roles with training that alerts them to their elevated risk and reviews the pertinent rules and procedures at the beginning of the dangerous period, you could have a much higher chance of winning their attention and changing their behavior. They know the data is watching, after all.

In such a situation, any training that provides clarity and peace of mind would become a welcome tool, and its lessons would be far more likely to be applied. Just imagine how powerful the email in Exhibit 12-1 could be in capturing the attention of a flagged individual. Wouldn't the recipient watch the subsequent training with at least a little added interest?

Exhibit 12-1. Compliance Email

To:	Employee Doe
Subject:	**Warning: Elevated Fraud Risk**

Message: Historical data indicates that your role has a 25 percent chance of engaging in a fraudulent behavior over the next 30 days. To ensure you are prepared to avoid that risk, please take the 10-minute prevention tutorial today to review the most common types and causes of fraud, as well as your core legal responsibilities.

Internal audit will continue using data science to monitor, reduce, and mitigate potential risks within the organization. If you have any questions, please don't hesitate to call at 123.456.7891.

Thank you for your continued commitment to a just, ethical, secure community. We couldn't reach our goals without you.

Senior Leadership

As an added benefit, predictive learning saves the rest of your population from a message that was likely irrelevant to them, without forfeiting any real risk reduction or mitigation in the process. One-size-fits-all compliance training may have been our best tool for managing risk in the past, given technological constraints, but those constraints are fading. Instead of subjecting all employees to a laboriously comprehensive set of preventive measures—measures that most will never even need—we can target future training initiatives exactly where the data says they are needed. That kind of targeted, data-driven plan is right in line with where the most progressive compliance laws are headed, and regulators' expectations for data are only likely to grow in the years ahead, as they see more examples of its power.

If we can demystify the unseen trends that generate misconduct in our organizations, we can create training that interrupts those trends and generates far different results. We can save time, improve transparency and trust, and reduce risk more than ever before. We only have to listen to our data and allow ourselves to act on its lessons.

The New Paradigm

If the last generation of business leaders asked how to maximize profits within legal and ethical constraints, the next generation promises to flip that question on its head. Thanks to technological advances and shifting societal expectations, ethics no longer has to be an afterthought. In fact, to enjoy sustainable organizational success in the climate of today and tomorrow, ethics must lead the parade.

Social media, open records, and blockchain technology will only continue to increase transparency, making misconduct impossible to hide and making its costs far more immediate to the organization's bottom line. But it's wrong to suggest that these new leaders will only be shifting to ethics for fear of being caught or publicly shamed. They will be shifting to ethics because they've always wanted to, and they finally can.

AI and other productivity tools promise to take over many of the reactionary tasks that consumed the daily calendars of managers and senior leaders in the past, allowing more time for proactive, strategic action in the future. If the last generation was forced to consider profit and process to stay afloat, automation will allow the next generation the time and financial freedom to consider what kind of people they want to be, and what kind of organizational cultures they want to build. Rather than robbing us of our humanity, technology might finally allow us to reach our full human potential.

Even if these bold predictions never quite come to fruition, existing developments in technology and culture have already begun shifting our employees' perspective and priorities. A survey of workers and college students found that 58 percent of the workforce would accept a pay cut if it meant working for a company that shared their values (Zukin and Szeltner 2012). Millennials likely aren't any more ethical than previous generations, but rising expectations of ethical employment, quality of life, and career prospects have certainly made it easier for our employees to voice their conscience with their wallets, and there's no reason to think that trend won't continue in the years ahead.

The worst thing we can do, as compliance training experts, is to fall too far behind that trend. If we continue lecturing to engaged, value-driven employees as if they are only a legal risk to be managed, we risk alienating the very people who could be raising our culture to new heights. If we keep conflating ethics with compliance, we risk cheapening the real values that our workforce wants us to champion, and missing real opportunities to bring those values to fruition. The sooner we can pivot to a values-based approach, the sooner we can begin realizing our employees' full potential.

Unfortunately, legal requirements are likely to lag behind our best efforts. Before we can leave traditional compliance training completely, we need politicians and regulators to improve laws and policies. We need mandates that allow organizations the freedom to look beyond universally required training, and instead pursue the initiatives that have the best chance of reducing risk. Instead of micromanaging training with hour or content requirements, we need behavioral targets and the freedom to hit those targets. Instead of dogmatic definitions for all, we need policies and training that are flexible enough to meet the needs of each audience and climate. We need room for real learning.

Required training is rarely a solution to any meaningful problem, but real, transformative learning can solve almost anything. Ultimately, we all—regulators, employees, lawmakers, managers, trainers, SMEs, CEOs, senior leaders, and the public—need to shift the conversation as far away as possible from concepts like compliance, requirements, and mandates. In their place, we must begin a long-overdue conversation about values, ethics, and responsibility.

While we wait for those necessary changes to take hold, behavioral compliance training can help fill the gap.

By following the tips in this book, you can create compliance training programs that meet the letter of every compliance mandate you face today. But by focusing those programs on real problems and real solutions, you can also win back the trust of your learners, eradicate the cynical perception of traditional compliance training, and lay the foundation for years of truly transformative change.

By building fully compliant training solutions—focused not just on your legal requirements, but also your learners and their needs—you can better protect your organization from the legal risks of misconduct today. Even more important, such training will prepare your organization to thrive in a world beyond compliance, ushering in a golden age of ethical leadership and values-based decision making in which your employees effectively regulate themselves and misconduct becomes largely a problem of the past.

Appendixes

Appendix 1
The Compliance Training Analysis Form

This form can be a critically important tool for balancing the letter of compliance laws and policies with the associated opportunities for behavior change within your organization. Fill the form out with your SME for a great head start on your next compliance training project.

SUBJECT TITLE	
AUDIENCE	
SOURCE *(Law or policy #, guidance letter, etc.)*	
CORE REQUIREMENTS *(What learning objectives or delivery formats are specifically required by the law or policy to which you are complying?)*	

How would you rate these requirements?	Strict and Specific ←→	Loose and Vague
STAKEHOLDERS Subject Matter Experts		
Legal Team		
Communications Team		
Training Manager and Colleagues		
Senior Leadership and Project Sponsors		

SPECIAL REQUIREMENTS *(Varying schedules, audience subsets, refresher options, legal signature requirements, etc.)*	

RELATED TRAINING NEEDS

(Related to this subject area, what real, observable training needs exist within your organization?)

Desired Behavior Change	Impact	Learnability
	High – Low	High – Low
	High – Low	High – Low
	High – Low	High – Low
	High – Low	High – Low
	High – Low	High – Low

Overall, how would you rate these learning needs?	Real and Relevant	←→	Forced and Irrelevant

MEASURABILITY

(What measures could you use to show whether your training achieves the desired behavior changes?)

1.	
2.	
3.	
4.	
5.	

ANALYSIS ASSESSMENT

(Building on everything you've learned in the analysis phase, in what quadrant would you place this compliance project?)

Training Needs — Relevant / Irrelevant

Specific | Vague

Compliance Requirements

Appendix 2
A Behavioral Training Plan Sample

The following training plan illustrates the relationship between outcomes, objectives, and behavioral levers, and could be used to satisfy the compliance requirements of nearly any data protection policy or law, with minor additions to meet specific requirements mandated by your regulatory environment. This may be a good foundation for an organization's GDPR training, for example.

Return to chapters 7-9 for further clarification on how a training initiative based on context, habit, and motivation can change behavior, along with further tips and tools for integrating the three levers into any compliance subject.

Compliance subject	Data Protection Law (FERPA, HIPPA, GDPR, etc.)
Behavioral outcome	Reduce the risk of a data breach.

Targeted Objectives by Role	
Role	**Programmers**
Long-term belief and culture change	When programmers are forced to choose between speed and security, they must instinctively prioritize security.
Short-term behavior change	When provisioning any new app, programmers should follow the full security checklist and resist the urge to skip steps when pressured by aggressive timelines.
Role	**Senior Leadership**
Long-term belief and culture change	When senior leadership considers the value of collecting or selling customer data, we need them to also consider the PR and legal risks of privacy infringement, as well as the risk of any potential data breaches.
Short-term behavior change	Project teams should complete a Data Awareness Questionnaire with a senior sponsor to ensure they collect data safely and legally, and that its value justifies the potential risk.
Role	**All Employees**
Long-term belief and culture change	When any member of staff encounters customer data—such as receipts, email addresses, phone numbers, or other personally identifiable information—they must sense the importance of that data and feel personal responsibility for it.
Short-term behavior change	Staff must be able to find and follow available protocols to ensure all forms of data are securely handled and kept for no longer than needed. In the moment of choice between moving on to the next customer or pausing to securely close out the files of the previous customer, staff must always choose to securely close out the previous files.

Behavioral Levers

Training to Change *Context*

1. To ensure the threat of a data breach remains front and center in the minds of all employees, staff will be required to watch a compelling three- to five-minute video on the human cost of failed data protection. The learner must feel the fear of a data breach viscerally for it to enter into their decision making in the moment of need.

2. Create a year-round training and communications plan—including signs, emails, videos, tutorials, follow-up surveys, and embedded system messages—to ensure that your data protection message remains an ever-present aspect of your employees' daily context.

3. Use train-the-trainer and data champion solutions to spread your data protection message through peers and trusted leaders in your organization, leveraging existing social networks. Establish the unifying branding message, "Data matters."

NOTE: Don't tell your learners the cost in regulatory terms or the money lost in legal settlements. That's too abstract and distant to alter their context in a meaningful or lasting way. Instead, tell a story about a single person terribly affected by a breach: The small business owner who saw his family business bankrupt by legal costs and settlements after losing his customer's credit card data; the programmer who lost his job for skimping on security; or the customer who still deals with the aftermath of a stolen identity decades after a breach. Those are the kind of stories that have a chance to stick.

Training to Change *Habit*

1. Examine the current habits that cause programmers to skip security protocols. Create new habit cycles by demonstrating and practicing improved routines that can achieve the same results when presented with the same cue in the future, but without the associated risk.

2. Use quick guides, embedded training, and other support tools to make the improved routine as easy to follow as possible.

3. Within this ongoing training and support, use the branding message "Data matters" to remind everyone of the human cost of a data breach and subtly reinforce that programmers can strive for a reward that includes completion of the task and the peace of mind of responsible security, instead of just settling for the lesser reward of mere completion.

Behavioral Levers

Training to Change *Motivation*

1. Create a half-day, minimally guided session for managers to explore the dilemma between the value of data and the risk of data, and challenge them to craft SOPs that best balance those twin needs. Once the purpose of the exercise is clear, provide sample dilemmas and allow your learners the autonomy to balance the needs as they see fit, within the constraints of the law.
2. Create a blended programmer course where each programmer is assigned a famous data breach to study in advance. Ask them to investigate the details and prepare a plan for avoiding similar breaches. Host an in-person session for them to share their findings with their peers.

Appendix 3
A GDPR Habit Case Study

The General Data Protection Regulation (GDPR) is a law enacted by the European Union in 2018 to regulate data protection standards and provide specific privacy protections for individuals within the European Union.

There are many specific regulations that comprise the new set of standards, and organizations that do business in the EU were busy in 2018 training nearly every employee on the ways daily business tasks would be affected by these stringent requirements.

To illustrate the power of a habit-based learning plan, we will explore one of the bad habits that GDPR singled out for action: the perpetual retention of resumes, and the sensitive data they contain, long after they are no longer needed.

It should be noted that employee records are just one component of GDPR, and hiring documents are just one of several kinds of employee records the law addresses. The key to habit-based learning, however, is not to lump everything in a single course. Instead, we must think of each new compliance mandate as a set of required habits, each likely to affect a different audience in response to different cues. If we are serious about behavior change, we must target our training initiatives at each habit, one at a time, addressing the behaviors we seek to change directly.

A collection of simple habit plans like the one shown here could do more to reduce risk and demonstrate commitment to GDPR than any long tutorial or in-person session ever could. It simply requires a shift in our definition of training, and an understanding of the core habits that drive behavior.

The Resume Retention Habit Plan

Current Behavior

Managers keep hiring documents forever, never revisiting the process once a hire is made.

Desired Behavior

Managers should keep resumes for six months following the hire, in case of complaints, and then delete them promptly to avoid unnecessarily stockpiling sensitive data that could be compromised.

Cue Modifications

When a new hire requisition is opened, managers are sent an email with a 30-second video explaining the reason for the required retention schedule. For example:

> We need documents for at least six months in case a hiring decision is challenged in court, but once that window passes, we must delete the information to preserve our applicant's privacy and avoid the risk of compromising their data at a later date.

Six months after the hire is finalized in the system, the manager receives a second email reminding them of their duty to delete the files. The email could also include the same video as the first email as an extra reminder of the importance of the task.

Routine Modifications

To make the right conduct easy, provide a quick guide to all managers and talent consultants for their immediate use, and remind them of the guide in the cue emails mentioned above. The quick guide will drill home a simple three-step routine:

1. Create a folder for every new position that you post to be filled.
2. Move all related documents to that folder throughout the selection process. If moving creates copies, delete the originals.

3. Add an event on your calendar for six months from the hire date, reminding you to delete the entire contents of the folder and formally end the hiring process.

Reward Modifications

Send a follow-up email one day after the initial reminder email is sent to delete the hiring documents. *Do not call this email a reminder.* Instead, thank your managers for the action they took yesterday to preserve the public trust in your organization, and congratulate them for responsibly managing their own personal liability by proactively deleting sensitive data.

This kind of email serves as a far more effective reminder for those who have forgotten to comply, and reminds all managers to associate their freshly completed routine with the intrinsic rewards of those routines: the satisfaction of completing one's responsibilities, and the peace of mind of removing a potential risk. Those are the kind of intrinsic rewards that are most likely to make your routine stick.

Bonus Reward

You can achieve more pervasive change by asking your managers how they could balance resume privacy requirements with the need to build candidate pools for future openings. GDPR guidance addresses that concern directly, with a process for obtaining an applicant's consent to be retained, but the results of the exercise are more meaningful and transformative if you let your managers develop their own solution. That kind of thoughtful exercise can begin to shape more universal habits—helping managers learn how to think about data privacy, and how to weave it into all aspects of their daily decision making.

Appendix 4

PBL Compliance Project Samples

Problem-based learning is a powerful tool for capturing our learners' motivation and inspiring them to practice ethical, effective skills and strategies that are likely to stick in the real world. The following three samples show how PBL techniques can be used to improve learner engagement and outcomes for different audiences and subjects.

The Risk Management Problem

Problem Statement

You are on the board of trustees for a Research 1 University and your organization is overwhelmed by the scope of modern compliance mandates. Review the current compliance landscape, assess your greatest areas of risk, and prepare a mitigation strategy for this fiscal year.

Audience
Senior leadership

Format
3-hour in-person session

Scaffolding and Resources

All groups receive comprehensive compliance binders with one-page summaries of your top 10 to 15 compliance subjects. The groups also have access to computers and SMEs to provide more detailed information as needed. Give each group three Compliance Training Worksheets, which will prompt them to identify genuine learning needs within their chosen subjects along with potential metrics for measuring behavior change.

Instructor Notes

1. Give a 10- to 15-minute overview of the modern compliance environment and the potentially catastrophic risks of noncompliance, as well as some compelling examples of inventive compliance learning.

2. Share two to three case studies of similar organizations that were found in breach of their compliance mandates and the consequences that ensued. Reveal that the key to surviving most compliance suits is a credible claim that the organization had been taking the demand seriously and moving earnestly toward a solution. Explain that this session is designed to help participants create a one-year plan that meets those requirements for their most pressing areas of need.

3. Break participants into small, representative groups of three to five executives.

4. Give each group a compliance binder and an overview of the available resources.

5. Provide ample time for each group to investigate their binders, identify the three compliance topics they believe pose the greatest risk, and complete the worksheets for each topic.

6. Have each group present their findings and a summary of their proposed training responses to the broader group.

7. After all groups have presented, have the full group vote on three to five compliance learning plans to put into action this year (choose a lower number if resources are limited).

Bonuses of This PBL Approach

Participating executives get a chance to model the strategic assessment and planning skills they need in their daily work, while also meeting their own individual compliance training requirements for the year. By collecting the worksheets at the end of class, you have much of the analysis phase complete for another round of relevant compliance programs, and you already have executive buy-in.

By repeating the experience year after year, you can keep your executives engaged in compliance and move toward a fully relevant library of compliance learning experiences.

By keeping the communication open between your team and the business's key decision makers, you can ensure your development resources remain focused on the most pressing and timely areas of need.

The Whistle-Blower Problem

Problem Statement

You are a new associate at a prestigious investment firm, and your manager and mentor is one of the most respected consultants in the business. However, a month into your position, you inadvertently discover that an internal audit is looking into your department's methods after reports that they may violate ethical regulations. You have to decide whether to defend your manager and stand by your practices or seek out and report additional information that may aid in the investigation.

Audience

Newly Hired Financial Associates

Format

1-hour scenario-based online tutorial

Scaffolding and Resources

The tutorial emphasizes the use of an online policy library employees can use to review policy summaries and details as needed. Ideally, this resource should be presented in a way that closely mimics or duplicates the real support tools participants can use back on the job. At key milestones, the learner is given limited branching options to help focus their decision making.

Instructor Notes

1.   Provide a brief five-minute opening that introduces the participants' role and relationship to the manager character. Conclude the opening with a clear call to action: The participants discover that their department is under investigation. A friend introduces them to the policy library and encourages them to use it to ensure they're not being asked to do anything that could expose the company to risk or jeopardize their position.

2. The bulk of the tutorial consists of three to five video scenarios where the participants observe or take direction from the manager character. Each video poses potentially troubling ethical implications, each representative of a different compliance mandate that applies to the financial sector.

3. The learners are given a choice of what do at the end of each scenario and encouraged to review the policy library as needed to reach the correct conclusion. If the learners need assistance navigating the library, they can ask the friend character for help in deciding what policy or policies might be most relevant to the situation. In some cases, the manager's behavior is acceptable. In others, it would violate a key policy. The learners' ability to interpret the facts and make fair decisions will be genuinely challenged by the options available at the end of each scenario.

4. At the end of the course, the learners are faced with a final decision: Based on the totality of the scenarios observed, will they report their concerns to the internal audit team or stand by their manager? The final outcome of the course varies by the selection made, reinforcing the participants' ability to make their own decisions, whether those decisions lead to success or failure.

Bonuses of This PBL Approach

The basic format allows for the natural integration of many separate financial compliance subjects within the sphere of one professional's daily experience. By situating each policy squarely in a complex real-world context, the audience learns not just the letter of the law, but also its purpose, implications, and challenges of interpretation.

And by building the course experience around the use of a realistic policy library, you equip your learners to utilize the resources available to them back in the office to ensure continued compliance over time, even as roles and regulations change. Even more importantly, you assuage your audience's whistle-blowing fears and prepare them to report unethical behavior should the need ever arise.

The Busy Warehouse Problem

Problem Statement

You work in a busy warehouse and you must fill a growing quota of orders each day without risking your personal safety or violating key safety policies.

Audience

Newly Hired Warehouse Workers

Format

1-hour video game experience

Scaffolding and Resources

All safety policies, guidelines, and best practices are shared during the course only as consequences to unsafe actions taken within the game. For example, if an employee launches a mission regarding a scissor lift without clicking to attach the safety harness, they may fall and sustain an injury or receive a reprimand from a boss. At the end of the experience, to ensure all compliance mandates are met, the employee is guided through the process of creating a step-by-step guide for the safety procedures they will commit to following back on the job. The learner will also be presented with links to all relevant safety laws and policies for their reference.

Instructor Notes

5. Learners are thrown immediately into a responsive video game environment where they can employ a few simple game mechanics to accomplish a range of progressively difficult tasks. As they complete each round, the number of goals they must complete increases, time decreases, and the game mechanics increase in complexity. For example, the learner may start the early levels on foot, but will need to operate a forklift or a scissor lift to succeed on later levels. The game need not be graphically advanced or overly complex, it simply has to allow continuous interaction with the environment and the possibility of fair success or failure.

6. Each time the learner chooses a new path or takes an action without observing an applicable safety procedure, he or she faces an in-game consequence like an injury or discipline. All relevant training is contained

within each of these consequences, as needed, including clear descriptions of what the learner should have done differently.

7. Similar scenarios are encountered throughout the game, but the game only pauses to deliver content when the learner makes a mistake.

8. As a debrief, at the end of the game, learners are given a list of the safety policies and laws that this training has prepared them to observe, along with direct links for future reference.

9. Learners are guided though generating a step-by-step safety guide that they will follow back in the office, either by dragging and dropping steps into a list or by typing out the steps from memory. If self-generated, the list should be checked automatically by text recognition software that prompts for forgotten steps, or reviewed by a manager or training administrator as a requirement for passing the course.

Bonuses of This PBL Approach

While game development can be costly and time consuming, the critical importance of safety may warrant the investment for many organizations. The game element places the entire focus of the experience squarely on behavior, with all learning confined in its natural context to increase the chance of recall later. If the mechanics are designed well enough, the experience can be repeated at regular intervals without frustrating the learner. As an added benefit, the accident statistics in later levels can be compared with those in earlier levels to provide metrics on the training's effectiveness, which can be linked more closely to actual behavior than simple pre- and post-learning quizzes.

References and Resources

Ahn, S.J., A.M.T. Le, J. Bailenson. 2013. "The Effect of Embodied Experiences on Self-Other Merging, Attitude, and Helping Behavior." *Media Psychology* 16:7-38. https://vhil.stanford.edu/mm/2013/ahn-mp-embodied-experiences.pdf.

Anderson, L.V. 2016. "Ethics Trainings Are Even Dumber Than You Think." *Slate,* May 16. https://slate.com/business/2016/05/ethics-compliance-training-is-a-waste-of-time-heres-why-you-have-to-do-it-anyway.html.

Asch, S.E. 1955. "Opinions and Social Pressure." *Scientific American* 193(5): 31-35.

Barraza, J.A., and P.J. Zak. 2009. "Values, Empathy, and Fairness Across Social Barriers." *New York Academy of Sciences* 1167: 182-189. www.nexthumanproject.com/references/Empathy_Towards_Strangers_Claremont.pdf.

Borrows, H.S., and R.M. Tamblyn. 1980. "Problem-Based Learning: An Approach to Medical Education." Vol. 1 in the Springer Series on Medical Education. New York: Springer.

Deci, E.L., R. Koestner, and R.M. Ryan. 1999. "A Meta-Analytic Review of Experiments Examining the Effects of Extrinsic Rewards on Intrinsic Motivation." *Psychological Bulletin* 125(6): 627.

EEOC (U.S. Equal Employment Opportunity Commission). 2016. "Task Force Co-Chairs Call on Employers and Others to 'Reboot' Harassment Prevention." Press Release, June 20. www.eeoc.gov/eeoc/newsroom/release/6-20-16.cfm.

Elder, A.D. 2019. "Using a Brief Form of Problem-Based Learning in a Research Methods Class: Perspectives of Instructor and Students." *Journal of University Teaching & Learning Practice* 12(1). http://ro.uow.edu.au/jutlp/vol12/iss1/8.

Fox, C.R. 1999. "Strength of Evidence, Judged Probability, and Choice Under Uncertainty." *Cognitive Psychology* 38:167-189. https://pdfs.semanticscholar.org/25b6/87fc03a8eb9910606cb75d3fd-0dae52e677a.pdf.

Fredeen, I. 2017. "2017 Ethics & Compliance Training Benchmark Report." Navex Global. www.navexglobal.com/sites/default/files/2017_Ethics_Compliance_Training_Benchmark_Report.PDF.

Kidd, D.C., and E. Castano. 2013. "Reading Literary Fiction Improves Theory of Mind." *Science* 342(6156): 377-380. https://scottbarrykaufman.com/wp-content/uploads/2013/10/Science-2013-Kidd-science.1239918.pdf.

McGregor, J. 2017. "Why Sexual Harassment Training Doesn't Stop Harassment." *Washington Post,* November 17. www.washington-post.com/news/on-leadership/wp/2017/11/17/why-sexual-harassment-training-doesnt-stop-harassment/?noredirect=on&utm_term=.cf3a20a49985.

Nodjimbadem, K. 2017. "The Trashy Beginnings of 'Don't Mess With Texas.'" *Smithsonian,* March 10. www.smithsonianmag.com/history/trashy-beginnings-dont-mess-texas-180962490.

Noguchi, Y. 2017. "Trainers, Lawyers Say Sexual Harassment Training Fails." NPR, *All Things Considered,* November 8. www.npr.org/2017/11/08/562641787trainers-lawyers-say-sexual-harassment-training-fails.

O'Connor, J. 2013. "Shark Phobia: The Memory of Jaws Continues to Scare Swimmers Away From the Ocean." *National Post,* March 2. https://nationalpost.com/news/shark-phobia-the-memory-of-jaws-continues-to-scare-swimmers-away-from-the-ocean.

Stein, M.L. 2017. "The Morning Risk Report: U.K. Enlists Behavioral Sciences to Fight Corruption." *Wall Street Journal,* December 19. https://blogs.wsj.com/riskandcompliance/2017/12/19/the-morning-risk-report-u-k-enlists-behavioral-sciences-to-fight-corruption.

U.S. DoJ (U.S. Department of Justice). n.d. "Evaluation of Corporate Compliance Programs." www.justice.gov/criminal-fraud/page/file/937501/download.

U.S. Sentencing Commission. 2004. "Commission Tightens Requirements for Corporate Compliance and Ethics Programs." Press Release, May 3. www.ussc.gov/about/news/press-releases/may-3-2004.

Warneken, F., and M. Tomasello. 2007. "Helping and Cooperation at 14 Months of Age." *Infancy* 11(3): 271-294.

Warneken, F., and M. Tomasello. 2008. "Extrinsic Rewards Undermine Altruistic Tendencies in 20-Month-Olds." *Developmental Psychology* 44(6): 1785.

Zukin, C., and M. Szeltner. 2012. "Talent Report: What Workers Want in 2012." Rutgers University, May. https://netimpact.org/sites/default/files/documents/what-workers-want-2012.pdf.

About the Author

Travis Waugh is an instructional designer, developer, speaker, and author with specialized interests in philosophy, psychology, technology, and law. He has spent the last 15 years creating relevant, timely learning programs for professionals in a variety of settings, from international language schools to corporate America and higher education. As a dedicated learning professional, Travis tries, above all else, never to waste anyone's time.

In his personal life, Travis is an avid sports fan, classic movie buff, and proud father of a one-year-old son. He is motivated by his dogged belief that people are generally good, and always worthy of good learning and development.

Index